White *as a* Ghost

● ● ● ● ● ● ● ● ● ● ●

Winter Ticks & Moose

BY BILL SAMUEL

Printed November 2004
Published by the Federation of Alberta Naturalists
11759 Groat Road, Edmonton, Alberta, T5M 3K6

Additional copies of this book, or any other FAN publication, may be obtained by contacting FAN at the above address.

Printed and Bound at Friesen Printers
Altona, Manitoba, Canada

MANAGING EDITOR: Glen Semenchuk, Executive Director, FAN

SERIES EDITOR: Dr. James A. Burns, Woolly Mammoth Services, Edmonton, Alberta

DESIGN AND ELECTRONIC LAYOUT: Judy Fushtey, Broken Arrow Solutions Inc., St. Albert, Alberta

MARKETING AND PUBLICITY: Lisa Monsees, Satori Communications, Edmonton, Alberta

COVER PHOTOGRAPH OF WHITE MOOSE: Rolf Peterson
COVER PHOTOGRAPH OF TICK: John and Leah Vucetich

Uncredited photos are property of the author. All others are appropriately credited.

CANADIAN CATALOGUING IN PUBLICATION DATA

Samuel, Bill, 1940-

    White as a ghost : winter ticks and moose / by Bill Samuel.

(Natural history series ; v. 1)

Includes bibliographical references and index.

ISBN 0-9696134-6-6

    1. Winter tick. 2. Moose—Parasites. I. Federation of Alberta Naturalists

II. Title. III. Series: Natural history series (Edmonton, Alta.) v. 1

QL458.2.I9S24 2004   595.4'29

C2004-906350-2

Dedicated to

The many outdoorsmen and women who embrace the outdoors of
Alberta: trappers, Fish and Wildlife officers, biologists, wildlife
managers, hunters and farmers; people like Cecil Cross, and
the too-soon-departed Mark Lynch, who respected and
loved the land, and had a first-hand knowledge
of ghost moose.

Ghost Moose

© 1993 Laura O'Neal

Just across the Canada line
this Grumman cuts water and moves with a glide.
All that we need to survive is here in this boat.

Not a chain away a male loon splashes
showing his wings to all who will see.
And answering off in the distance she chooses her call.

And slowly the land becomes islands and the
northern lights dance in the sky.
And in the bogs on these islands the crazy moose madden
crazy from the pain.

A mile long portage can break your back
but secretly you ask for the pain.
You bring it on yourself a challenge to conquer
And its done with the shimmer of the water.

Cozy in the tent but nervous as a smoker
something with great weight is crashing all around.
No sleep for the fear of a hoof in the head
And we clutch to the promise of morning

While slowly the land becomes islands and the
northern lights dance in the sky.
And in the bogs on these islands the crazy moose madden
Crazy from the pain.

So we dab on our repellent and pull down the netting.
And use our five digits to check for the crawlies,
That frighten the Ghost Moose,
He's itchy from the tick chomp.

While slowly the land becomes islands and the
northern lights dance in the sky.
And in the bogs on these islands the crazy moose madden
Crazy from the pain. The wildest of the wild gone mad.

Table of Contents

normal winter activities like eating and resting. About this time, patches of shed and broken hair and drops of blood could be observed on snow wherever the calf travelled or rested. The hair coat began disappearing from the side of the neck and along the shoulder and flank. Life was taking a serious turn.

Then, in late March, the close bond between cow and her calf began to break down. The cow, like her calf, had acquired a significant number of winter ticks and went from intensive grooming that damaged her coat of hair (FIGURE 1), to acting lethargically. Life for her was also taking a serious turn. In fact she had thousands of blood-feeding winter ticks deriving nourishment from her body and robbing her of energy desperately needed to grow her two unborn fetuses. Her calf of last year was soon forgotten.

FIGURE 1. The cow moose, with tattered hair coat, was showing signs of winter tick infestation. [MARK DREW]

In the best of winters, food quality and quantity can be limited for moose in March and April. Much of the most

nutritious and preferred vegetation has been consumed and moose appear to be "hanging on" until new green growth arrives. Owing to this and the added burden of dealing with feeding winter ticks, the calf began to weaken. As so often happens in the wild, one bad thing was leading to another.

Bloodstains were clearly visible on snow wherever the moose walked or bedded. The calf grew weaker by the day. Large, grey-to-pale blue ticks, the size of small grapes, began dropping from the calf. Magpies looking for a good source of protein landed on the back of the calf, or on the snow next to the bedded animal and ate ticks until full, then cached many others in leaf litter for future meals.

The calf spent long periods of time standing, seeming to stare aimlessly into space. The realities of its world were growing distant.

In early April, a young farmer noticed the calf as it moved slowly along the edge of one of his cut grain fields. He approached the calf to within a few metres and noted that it was gaunt, with a tattered hair coat. In fact, he noticed that much hair was completely gone; dark, crusted skin was easily observed. Other hair, particularly on the neck, shoulder, rib cage and around the anus, had been broken at the base giving the animal a whitish appearance.

The young man had a sense of foreboding as he realized the calf was near death. "This calf is soon done", he sighed to himself. "Strange-looking, too; looks ghostly."

He had heard of the "ghost" moose from his father, who had first broken the soil where he now farmed. One year previous, he had seen such a moose in the distance, but he had never seen one close-up.

Backtracking hoof prints in the snow, the farmer found where the calf had rested earlier. Much blood and shed hair were present in the snow at the bed site. He also noticed some grape-like things in the snow; they proved to be ticks. He crushed one between his fingers and the blood spurted.

Two days later he found the calf dead along the edge of the field (FIGURE 2).

Moose populations are doing well in North America, but this scene is repeated often and annually in Alberta and throughout much of the Canadian range of moose. In some years many moose are involved, in other years, few moose. What follows is a summary of the unique, maybe even amazing, relationship between moose and winter ticks.[1]

FIGURE 2. Calf moose victim of winter ticks.
[INSET, ROLF PETERSON]

---

[1] The main players in the story are moose (scientific name: *Alces alces*) and winter tick (*Dermacentor albipictus*).

The winter tick is a serious pest of moose. [JOHN AND LEAH VUCETICH]

What makes ticks *tick?*

Most animals, be they domestic or wild, pets or humans, become host to parasites at least sometime during their life. Chances are most of us have been infected with at least one parasite or another. Did you or your children acquire pinworms, a roundworm, or head lice when you/they were young? Many do. It is a wormy world.

I remember well when my 5-year-old son acquired pinworms and how agitated my spouse became when I collected pinworm eggs from around his anus using scotch tape! The technique works well because the female pinworm, usually found associated with mucosa of the large intestine, commonly crawls to the anal region laying eggs as she goes. Sticky eggs are found on sheets, nearby walls, toothbrushes and on soiled fingers of thumb-sucking youngsters during the night. It is actually hard not to become infected, or reinfected, in a contaminated household. But back to the scotch tape, which picks up eggs shed in the anal region during the night. The opportunity to collect some eggs for

The world is ticky and there are not many nice things one can say about ticks. As you will see, the word *tick* makes for some neat puns, but otherwise, humour tends to be lost on these rascals.

our parasite collection at the university was too good to pass, but doing this before purchasing medication at the drugstore did not go over well!

Parasites are small organisms that live in or on another organism called the host, and derive nourishment from that organism. More scientifically, parasitism is the association between two populations of organisms, the smaller of which, the parasite, is physiologically dependent on the larger, the host.

The relationship between parasite and host can be thought of as an "arms race". Thus, in a typical interaction between a parasite and its vertebrate host, the parasite uses a variety of adaptations, some structural, others behavioural, to acquire a host and to survive and reproduce successfully on or in that host. The host, in turn, has evolved a variety of defences, some behavioural, others immunological, against parasite attack. These defences help regulate numbers of parasites. In general, given good nutrition and appropriate densities of animals on the landscape, wild and domestic hosts and their parasites get along well. There is equilibrium between parasite and host wherein numbers of parasites are relatively few on or in most hosts, and death of hosts is rare. But as you will see later, sometimes things go wrong (FIGURE 1.1).

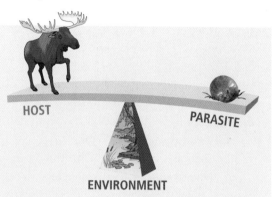

FIGURE 1.1. One can think of the equilibrium that exists in most host-parasite relationships, wherein host and parasite usually co-exist quite well, as a teeter-totter with the environment as a fulcrum.

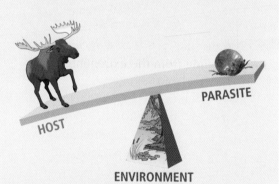

This delicate balance can be thrown out of kilter when there is a change in the environment—say, a bad winter—that puts stress on the host's food supply and moves the fulcrum to favour the parasite. Host resistance then works to fight the infection and rebalance the relationship.

There are two types of parasites: those that live in the host—the endoparasites such as the pinworms just mentioned—and those that live on the host, the ectoparasites. Ticks are ectoparasites.

The world is ticky and there are not many nice things one can say about ticks. As you will see, the word tick makes for some neat puns, but otherwise, humour tends to be lost on these rascals. Ticks go back a long way. If you search the web for information, you will find that Aristotle referred to ticks as "disgusting parasitic animals". I have not been able to confirm this quote, but it makes good sense. To this day, not much has changed. In fact the more we learn about ticks, the more disgusting they appear to be. Well, not quite. There is one group of scientists, the parasitologists, who study the world of parasites and who do not call ticks disgusting. To parasitologists, especially those who study ticks, the acarologists, ticks are fascinating creatures due to their unique life style and the many disorders they cause and diseases they transmit.

All ticks feed on blood and tissue fluids and therein lies the problem. As they feed they not only remove blood, but also cause local irritation at the site of feeding and introduce a variety of pathogens to the host. Pathogens vectored by ticks include viruses, and bacteria such as the rickettsias, which cause diseases such as Rocky Mountain spotted fever, and the spirochetes that cause Lyme disease.

■ Characteris-*ticks*

Ticks belong to a huge group of organisms known as arthropods. The arthropods comprise the largest (as in several million species) and most diverse phylum of organisms on earth. They are invertebrates with segmented bodies, jointed appendages and a body surface covered by a chitinous cuticle called an exoskeleton. You know the arthropods as insects, spiders, crustaceans and others. And one of the "others" is ticks. Unlike insects, ticks have four pairs of legs (insects have three) and lack antennae and divided body.

Rather, ticks have a saclike leathery appearance, with a tiny head, which consists of elaborate mouthparts, and the body, which is comprised mostly of the abdomen. Ticks basically look like a body with four pairs of legs (FIGURE 1.2).

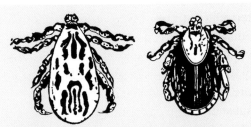

FIGURE 1.2. Winter ticks have a sac-like leathery appearance, with fused head (basically, head = elaborate mouthparts), body and abdomen. The adult male on the left has white markings on a reddish brown background. The adult female is reddish brown.

Ticks are common parasites of mammals, including humans. Some species are also found on birds and reptiles. There are over 800 species of ticks worldwide, but only about 35 species occur on hosts in Canada. Of that number only 10 or so occur in Alberta, and of those few, only two get much attention.[2]

The Rocky Mountain wood tick, *Dermacentor andersoni*, occurs on large mammals such as deer,[3] elk,[4] cattle and humans from south central British Columbia, southern and western Alberta, and east to southwestern Saskatchewan. This tick deserves the attention it gets because hikers and dogs, walking game trails, commonly become infested in spring and early summer and disease can result.

Wood ticks ascend grasses and shrubs along game trails and ambush large

mammals including man. They occur in Alberta's foothills and mountains from Jasper to the Montana border (Brown, 1944; Brown and Kohls, 1950; Wilkinson, 1967). Basically, where elk, mule deer and bighorn sheep are found, so too are wood ticks. Moving east in Alberta, wood ticks occur south of a west-east line running through Lake Louise and Hanna.

Wood ticks vector the human disease Rocky Mountain spotted fever that, in spite of its name, is not very common in Alberta, but rather reaches near epidemic proportions in dogs of the southeastern Atlantic states.[5] The disease, which first produces a mild-to-nasty skin rash often accompanied by headache, fever, general soreness, then more severe signs later such as agitation and insomnia, is readily treated with antibiotics.

A second ailment is tick paralysis, which occurs rarely in humans or other animals in Alberta, but is more common in cattle of British Columbia. Ticks produce a neurological toxin that is passed to hosts, such as cattle and man, during tick bite. Infection results in a gradually spreading loss of feeling from the extremities to the body core.

In summary, getting ambushed by wood ticks is part of hiking in southern and western Alberta in spring, but infection with spotted fever or tick paralysis is rare. Nonetheless, these diseases can be serious, which merits taking precautions to reduce chances of tick attack:

- avoid resting (that is, sitting or lying down) along game trails or mountain meadows obviously frequented by

---

[2] In 2002, Dr. Terry Galloway, University of Manitoba, wrote a great little popular article on ticks of the Canadian prairies. It appeared in *Blue Jay*, a journal published by Nature Saskatchewan, Regina, Saskatchewan. (I provide the full reference in the Bibliography).

[3] Mule deer, *Odocoileus hemionus*, are the most likely deer to be infected in Alberta, but white-tailed deer, *Odocoileus virginianus*, are now also common in the foothills of western Alberta.

[4] The term elk will be used in this text as the common name for the North American wapiti, *Cervus elaphus*.

[5] The main tick vector in eastern regions of North America is the dog tick, *Dermacentor variabilis*.

deer, elk or bighorn sheep (their poop, often in the form of pelleted groups on the ground, gives them away!);

- use repellents containing DEET on clothing below the waist, that is, those areas that might come into contact with low-lying tick-infested vegetation;
- tuck pants into the socks;
- do a body search for ticks of everyone in the hiking party during and at the end of the day. Search everyone for ticks, especially young children. It takes several to many hours for disease transmission to occur, so these searches are worthwhile. Wood ticks tend to attach around the ears and back of the neck, often just under the hairline. Check the dog.

If an attached tick is found, use tweezers to grasp the tick as close to the skin as possible and gently pull so as to remove both tick and its mouthparts. By the way, the many home-spun remedies for removing attached ticks, such as using nail polish, the end of a lit cigarette or hot match, petroleum jelly, or lighter fluid, do not work. Treat the site with antiseptic. See a physician if you are not certain that the mouthparts have been removed (and one sign that they have not been removed is inflammation at the site of the attached tick), or if you do not feel well following the hike.

The second attention-getting species of tick in Alberta is called the moose-, elk- or winter tick, *Dermacentor albipictus* (FIGURE 1.3). The common names refer to the hosts on which the tick is noticed most often and the season in which these ticks are observed most often. Humans are seldom, if ever, infested with winter ticks; this tick is not considered a pest of man.

You might think that ticks would be highly visible on moose or elk in winter, but they are not, remaining hidden in the thick winter coat of hair. However, one can easily recognize a ticky moose or elk by the characteristic pattern of hair loss caused by the feeding ticks. Biting ticks cause the sensation of itch, and moose and elk scratch the itch by grooming with their tongue and hooves and rubbing against standing and downed trees. Extensive grooming by both moose and elk produces a characteristic, tick-induced pattern of damage to the hair coat.

For years, rural Canadians in moose country have termed moose with severe damage to, and loss of, the winter hair coat caused by winter ticks "ghost moose" in recognition of their ghost-like appearance (FIGURE 1.4). There is only one cause of this condition: winter ticks.

FIGURE 1.3. The three main hosts for winter ticks in Alberta and much of North America are moose (*Alces alces*), elk (*Cervus elaphus*) and white-tailed deer (*Odocoileus virginianus*).

FIGURE 1.4. Aerial view of a "ghost" moose. The ghost appearance is caused by infestation of winter ticks, which causes moose to groom, thus breaking off much hair and creating the white appearance. [MARK DREW].

Tick-infested elk suffer less, but have a notch or collar of hair damage at the base of the neck (FIGURE 1.5).

The scientific name of the winter tick, *Dermacentor albipictus*, is derived from several Greek or Latin words. *Derma* is Greek for "the skin". *Centor* comes from the Greek word *kentein* meaning "to prick or stab". And ticks do just that. They prick the skin. *Albi* is derived from the Latin word *albus*, meaning "white". And *pictus*

is from the Latin word *pingere* meaning "to paint".[6] This makes sense in that it looks like someone has painted white lines on a reddish-brown background on the dorsal side or "back" of the adult male.

■ Gigan-*tick*

As ticks go, the adult winter tick is large. Adult females can be up to 1.5 centimetres long (3/4 inch) and weigh just less than 1 gram after feeding on blood of their host. Winter ticks occur on many species of large mammals in North America. Hoofed mammals (the ungulates), particularly members of the deer family, are the main hosts. This includes moose, elk, white-tailed and mule deer, and woodland caribou. The primary domestic hosts are horses and cattle. Other incidental wildlife hosts include beaver, mountain sheep, mountain goat, bison, pronghorn, black bear, coyote and wolf. The latter-listed carnivores likely acquire winter ticks while feeding on the carcass of a tick-infested moose, elk or woodland caribou in late winter or early spring.

FIGURE 1.5. Tick-infested calf elk with characteristic notch of broken hair at base of neck. This damage results from elk using hooves (hind leg) to scratch the area. Most elk in Alberta's mountain parks show these lesions in late winter.

[6] Dr. James Kierans, a leading tick specialist and professor at Georgia Southern University, provided information on the derivation of *pictus*.

Thin moose in June recovering from what must have been a heavy infestation of ticks. [JOHN AND LEAH VUCETICH]

Winter tick history:
A chronology of tick problems

There are 33 species of parasites known from North American moose. Three garner the most attention by far: a pathogenic nematode called meningeal worm (often called brainworm), which kills moose in eastern Canada, the large American liver fluke, and winter ticks. (More on brainworm and liver fluke later.) The winter tick, with much broader geographic distribution on moose than meningeal worm or liver fluke, probably ranks as the most important pest of moose.

A. S. Packard described the winter tick in 1869, from ticks sent to him by a Mr. W. J. Hays who discovered them on two captive moose brought through New York City on their way to Europe. The moose had been raised in Nova Scotia and were tame. Summaries of winter ticks causing problems for moose begin the year winter tick was described in 1869. In that year, Hardy stated that winter ticks were an irritant to moose in winter and early spring and were often seen on the snow where moose had lain (paraphrased from a quote seen in a 1974 review of moose parasites and

diseases by R. C. Anderson and M. W. Lankester).

Summaries of winter ticks causing problems for moose begin the year winter tick was described in 1869.

■ Tiny tick–giant killer

Although direct evidence of the lethal effect of winter ticks on moose populations is lacking, there is some important experimental evidence, along with observational and other field studies, supporting the idea that winter ticks kill many moose. What follows is a chronological summary of published records of ticks causing problems for wild moose.

■ 1900-1930

In his classic 1909 series of books, *Lives of Game Animals*, Ernest Thompson Seton stated that winter tick was an "enemy" of moose. From then to now, there are many undocumented and documented reports of dead and dying moose in late winter and early spring with extensive damage to the winter coat of hair and with many winter ticks. These reports come from many areas in Alberta, British Columbia, Idaho, Maine, Manitoba, Minnesota,

New Brunswick, New Hampshire, Nova Scotia, Ontario, Saskatchewan, Vermont and Wyoming.

Dymond and colleagues (1928) mentioned that the first recorded die-off of moose appeared in the 1916 *Report of the Chief Game Guardian,* published by the Saskatchewan Department of Agriculture, Regina. Winter ticks were thought responsible for the death of many moose in northern Saskatchewan in the spring of 1916. Dymond also records a moose die-off in the Lake Nipigon region of northwestern Ontario in 1922, and large numbers of moose died near the village of Gull Bay. Residents believed the loss to be due to ticks. In Saskatchewan a tick-associated die-off was reported in winter 1921-1922 (Cameron and Fulton, 1926-1927). Many horses and cattle died as well. Apparently, numbers of moose and winter ticks had been increasing in preceding years. Fenstermacher and Jellison (1933) report a die-off of tick-infested moose in the spring of 1923 near Moose Lake, Minnesota, in Lake County near the Canadian border.

■ 1930-1960

Twelve moose were found dead in the winter of 1931-1932 in Superior National Forest of Minnesota. Nine were necropsied and the report of Fenstermacher and Jellison (1933) reads as follows:

> "All the moose except one that were examined after death had been infested more or less by the winter ticks *Dermacentor albipictus* Packard. Some had been so badly infested that not a single place was found in the areas frequented by ticks that were

not covered with them. The skin is without hair in many places, particularly on the shoulders, ventral and lateral sides of the abdomen, the pectoral and inguinal regions, the medial surface of the femoral region and the posterior surface of the hind limbs and the anus. Wherever it is possible for the moose to rub against objects, the hair had usually been worn off. The skin in these areas has a thick, leathery appearance similar in some respects to that of cattle affected with mange. Dried blood was found adhering to the skin. Blood may sometimes be seen along the trails and on windfalls frequented by tick-infested moose. Blood is occasionally found in their beds…The favorite locations of the ticks are around the anus, the inguinal region, sternum, inner parts of the conchal cartilage,[8] over the withers, and down further on the shoulders."

Other tick-related die-offs of moose were reported from Nova Scotia (1930-1935), New Brunswick (early 1930s) and Ontario (1933-1939).

In the 1933 Alberta *Report of the Game Commissioner,* S. H. Clark mentioned the loss of many moose to ticks during the harsh winter of 1932-1933. In the next annual report, Clark stated: "Moose found in a dying condition [between Pembina and Athabasca rivers] were covered with ticks."

Blyth and Hudson (1987) reviewed the chronology of tick-influenced die-offs of moose in Elk Island National Park, central Alberta. Elk Island National

---

[8] "Choncha" is used in anatomical nomenclature to designate a structure that looks shell-like, in this case almost certainly the ear.

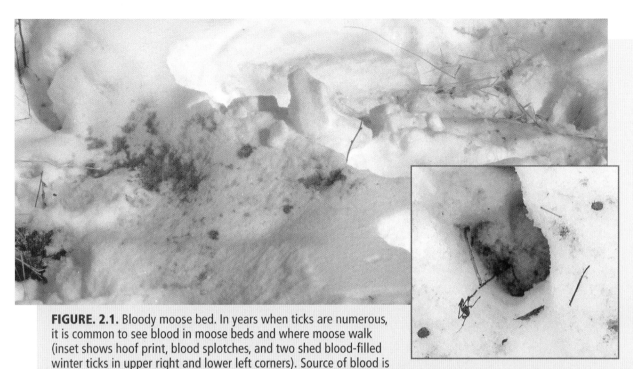

FIGURE. 2.1. Bloody moose bed. In years when ticks are numerous, it is common to see blood in moose beds and where moose walk (inset shows hoof print, blood splotches, and two shed blood-filled winter ticks in upper right and lower left corners). Source of blood is likely from dried blood in tick feces, open wounds at sites where feeding female ticks have just dropped from moose, and from ruptured live ticks that get crushed as moose moves in, or rises from, its frozen bed. [PARKS CANADA, ELK ISLAND NATIONAL PARK].

Park is 195 square kilometres (75 square miles) of aspen forest vegetation situated between Alberta's prairies to the south and boreal forest to the north. It lies just east of Edmonton in the Beaver Hills and is surrounded by a 2.2-metre (7-foot)-high paige wire ungulate fence. Moose died in winters 1931-1932 and 1932-1933 with no mention of tick problems.[9] Moose and elk died in winter 1935-1936 with park staff clearly associating mortality with the presence of ticks. Most moose showed hair loss in spring of 1937, in what was described as a "bad tick infestation" by the park's superintendent. All moose were heavily infested with ticks in the spring of 1938 and many moose died. The outbreak continued to 1939. Other major tick-related die-offs occurred in the park in 1947-1948, 1968-1969, 1977-1982, 1988-1990 and 1991-1992.

Severe infestations of ticks were reported from moose in other national parks of western Canada in the winter of 1942-1943, a very severe winter. Dr. Ian McTaggart Cowan, eminent wildlife biologist, then professor from University of British Columbia, suggested (1951) that moose ticks were important because they tended to attack young animals during periods of food shortage and severe weather. He also noted that wounds left by feeding ticks in March and April bled freely and the animal's trail in the snow was spotted with blood. Shaking moose would spatter blood over "several feet" and every moose bed was "blood-soaked" (SEE FIGURE 2.1). The stronger animals

---

[9] In his Master of Science thesis, Blyth (1995) said: "Each outbreak [of winter ticks – peak years for ticks were 1933, 1937, 1948, 1968, and 1981 based on reports of tick-caused alopecia (loss of hair) on moose] occurred after rapid increases in moose numbers and in each case significant tick numbers and alopecia were associated with subsequent population declines."

recovered, the weaker moose died. Cowan concluded that winter ticks are "the most harmful of all moose parasites and probably cause more losses than all other parasites and diseases combined". He also mentioned that many elk died from tick attack in the southern Rocky Mountains in some winters (for example, 1943-1944).

D. E. Forstad stated in the 1946-1947 Alberta *Report of the Game Superintendent*: "The moose tick has undoubtedly caused a tremendous amount of damage to this big game animal, reducing as it does the vitality and resistance of the animal so that it cannot survive a severe winter. There is no doubt but some special regulations will sooner or later have to be enacted to take care of the dwindling moose population."

Some of the most interesting reading on a qualitative assessment of winter ticks affecting moose is found in James Hatter's 1950 doctoral thesis. Hatter wrote of heavy infestations in central British Columbia beginning around 1942 and peaking from 1945 to 1948. He reported that 152 and 215 moose were found dead in central British Columbia in the late winter and early spring of 1947 and 1948, respectively, apparently all heavily tick-infested. He attributed losses to a "winter tick-malnutrition complex".

In one chapter of his thesis, Hatter recorded daily activity of an adult cow in central British Columbia beginning March 14, 1948. On that date the cow looked fine except for tick-induced hair loss on its left shoulder. On March 16, "...the cow spent a full hour in rubbing against small trees in order to relieve the irritation set up by the ticks. She deliberately walked beneath leaning trees in order to scratch the skin along the spinal region". More of the shoulder and neck were bare by April 4. Engorged ticks were numerous around the anus and along the inguinal region to the belly.

Ritcey and Edwards (1958) observed "heavy tick loads" on moose in central British Columbia in the winters of 1952 and 1953. One bull was tracked 275 metres (300 yards) in the snow as it moved and rested in two beds, and 240 adult, blood-fed winter ticks were recovered along the way. One of their conclusions was that ticks alone do not seriously weaken moose, but malnourished or old moose might host many ticks.

FIGURE 2.2. Calves with many ticks die of exposure during snowstorms in late winter or early spring.

1960-1990

Berg (1975) reported that a die-off of moose, mostly calves, occurred during a late winter blizzard and sub-zero temperatures in northwestern Minnesota in March 1974 (FIGURE 2.2). Cause of mortality was attributed to exposure in poor habitats, in conjunction with heavy winter tick infestations.

In 1979, leading authority on the interaction of moose and winter ticks, Dr. Ed Addison, then with the Ontario Department of Natural Resources, documented a 1979 outbreak of winter ticks on moose in Alfred Bog, an agricultural area of southeastern Ontario. The moose population had dropped from approximately 85 to 45 in this area between 1978 and 1979. Addison examined five moose found dead on March 15, 1979. All had winter ticks; two had an estimated 83,000 and 86,000! Dr. Addison concluded that, although the exact cause of death of these moose was unknown, it certainly appeared that winter ticks were involved. Other factors were mentioned such as harassment by snowmobilers and the "bitter cold" weather. Adding a historical note dealing with the many undocumented reports of dead moose heavily infested with winter ticks in late winter, Addison mentioned that "…during the spring of 1956, a trapper in the Kirkland Lake District of Ontario found 37 dead moose while routinely checking his trapline in Coulson and Beatty townships near Matheson".

The winter of 1981-1982 Samuel and Barker (1979) reported an estimated 100 moose died in Elk Island National Park in March and April of 1977. Approximately 20 dead moose were found, all heavily infested with winter ticks. The winter of 1981-1982 was particularly hard on moose in the Park. Moose numbers in the north side of Elk Island Park exceeded 350 the previous 2 years; temperatures were cold; snow was approximately 50 centimetres in depth, deep but not too deep for moose. Nine moose (8 adults and 1 calf) were shot and 10 others (3 adults and 7 calves) were found dead; many other weak, tick-riddled moose were seen (FIGURE 2.3). Tick numbers had been building in previous years; the average number the previous winter was 44,840 per moose. The average number for the 10 moose found dead was 82,880 per moose, or 4.6 ticks per square centimetre of skin

FIGURE 2.3. Often, more calves than adults die during tick-associated die-offs of moose. [PARKS CANADA, ELK ISLAND NATIONAL PARK].

surface. Numbers for the nine moose shot averaged 43,088 per moose, or 1.8 ticks per square centimetre of skin surface. (Later you will see that the problems ticks cause moose are a direct function of tick numbers. More ticks, more problems.)

Many tick-covered moose died that winter in other parts of Alberta and elsewhere. In fact, in 1983 the *Toronto Globe and Mail* stated: "A severe tick infestation in one area of the Omineca-Peace region [northern British Columbia] is being blamed in part, for an estimated 30 percent mortality rate among moose since 1979, according to biologist Fred Harper."

Tick related die-offs of moose were widespread in North America from 1988 to 1990 and were reported from Elk Island Park, Isle Royale National Park, north-central Ontario, Manitoba and northeastern Minnesota.

Dr. Rolf Peterson, Michigan Technological University, has studied moose-wolf interactions for many years at Isle Royale National Park, an island park off the coast of northeastern Minnesota in Lake Superior near Thunder Bay, Ontario. As wolves began decreasing in the 1980s, winter ticks appeared to become more important as agents of mortality. Statements of observation (Peterson, 1990, 1991; Peterson and Vucetich, 2003) include:

- "Presently, winter ticks, driven by weather, probably rival wolves as a regulating influence for the moose population."
- "This small creature [the winter tick] may compensate, in some respects at least, for the reduced presence of wolves."
- "A substantial die-off of moose occurred in late winter and spring, 1989, and the frequency of tick-loaded carcasses was unlike

anything witnessed at Isle Royale in the past 30 years."

A front-page article in the *Duluth News-Tribune*, March 15, 1991, titled "Tick outbreak cuts moose population by half", suggested that ticks were the main mortality factor in the loss of half the 6700 moose counted in northeastern Minnesota in 1989.

■ 1990-present

Thanks to good record keeping in Elk Island National Park, peak tick infestations (based on numbers of reports of tick-induced hair loss) and minor or major die-offs of moose are recorded for 1932-1938, 1948, 1968, 1977-1982, 1988-1990, and 1992.

Tick-related die-offs of moose recorded since 1990 include Minnesota (1991, 1996, 1999), Algonquin Provincial Park, Ontario (1992, 1999), Vermont (1992), and Alberta, British Columbia, Manitoba, New Brunswick, Ontario and Saskatchewan (1999). The most recent tick-related die-offs occurred in 2002 in New Hampshire, Vermont and Maine, Alberta, Saskatchewan and Manitoba, and Isle Royale National Park, Minnesota. These die-offs involved many thousands of moose.

Lenarz (1992) reported a major "tick-related" moose die-off in 1991 in northeastern Minnesota. Forty-six percent of moose observed in March 1991 had visible tick-caused loss of the winter hair coat.

Garner and Wilton (1993) reported major losses of moose in Algonquin Provincial Park, Ontario, in winter 1992; 43 carcasses with either heavy tick infestations or severe tick-induced loss of winter hair were found during routine field activities. Biologists in the Park recorded the highest proportion of moose ever observed with severe loss of hair. Similarly, more apparently tick-related deaths in moose were observed than in any previous year. The authors concluded that winter ticks were an important cause of moose mortality. They found a much higher than usual number of stillborn calves in 1992, indicating stress of ticks on pregnant cow moose.

In 1999 there was what has been termed a "Canada-wide epidemic of winter ticks in moose", accompanied by losses of many thousands of moose. Approximately 1000 of the 5000 moose in Riding Mountain National Park, Manitoba died, this attributed to an unusually high infestation of ticks.[10] Garner and Wilton (1993) reported that many moose died in Algonquin Provincial Park in winter, 1992.

During the major tick-associated die-off of moose in Alberta in 1999, Dr. Margo Pybus, wildlife disease specialist with Alberta Department of Sustainable Resource Development, collated and published data collected by field biologists and officers. She summarized the number of occurrences in winter 1999 in which field officers or biologists either directly handled moose or received phone calls about moose in distress, or situations when moose created concern for public safety. An unusually high number (1130) of moose occurrences was documented. Of those, 1035 moose were reported to have damaged hair coats caused by ticks and 311, or 28%, involved dead moose. Most occurrences were within the boreal habitats of northern and western Alberta. Dr. Pybus stated that the outbreak was the direct result of the interactions among moose, ticks, habitat and weather.

In March and April, 1999, I visited 18 moose carcasses near Edmonton. All had winter ticks and tick-caused loss of the winter hair coat. Thirteen were calves.

Dr. Helen Schwantje, wildlife veterinarian, British Columbia Ministry of Environment, Lands and Parks, provided anecdotal notes from regional officers in central interior and northeastern British Columbia that indicate a major tick-related die-off also occurred in British Columbia in 1999. Field staff reported:

- "huge" tick loads and much moose mortality from McBride to Valemont;
- farmers complaining of moose damage to stacks of hay with some moose entering barns and sheds seeking protection from the elements;
- blood in moose beds;
- "In my 25 years in the north, I have never seen the numbers of dead moose we have seen this year.";
- "The Prince George and area moose population is experiencing one of the worst tick infestations in recent history. Many of these hairless moose are wandering into human habitation and are causing a great deal of public concern."

There were losses of moose in certain regions of western Canada (Samuel and Crichton 2003), Maine, New Hampshire, Vermont and Isle Royale National Park in winter-spring 2002.[11] Losses were relatively low in British Columbia and Alberta, compared with 1999, but high in Saskatchewan and Manitoba.

---

[10] Comments of Marvin Miller, Chief Warden of the Park, in *National Post* article by Adam Killick, April 27, 1999.

[11] *High moose mortality from winter tick—Spring 2003.* Wildlife Health Centre Newsletter, vol. 9, no. 1: 9 (Winter Issue). Compiled by Bill Samuel, Vince Crichton and Ted Leighton from information gathered by a variety of investigators including Bill Samuel (University of Alberta), Vince Crichton (Manitoba Conservation), Ted Leighton (Canadian Cooperative Wildlife Health Centre), Margo Pybus (Alberta Sustainable Resource Development) and Helen Schwantje (British Columbia Wildlife).

In Alberta, mortality was concentrated along the southern fringe of the boreal forest, in central aspen parklands, and in the usual hotspot regions of the northwest, near the towns of Peace River and Grande Prairie. Hair loss was significant; tick numbers and moose mortality were high. In 2002 the Edmonton area experienced the coldest April in approximately 50 years, with large amounts of wet snow. Many calves died, most in late April and well into May. I examined a calf that died April 19 with engorged female ticks lined up like shingles on a roof on much of the chest, neck, lateral sides, abdomen and other ventral surfaces, and inguinal area.

Losses in Saskatchewan were concentrated in east-central regions (for example, Porcupine Plain area). Conservation Officer Ty Andrychuk reported at least 50 dead, tick-laden moose in Greenwater Provincial Park and area. As is often seen in early spring die-offs, moose were found in towns (FIGURES 2.4 and 2.5), woodsheds, under decks, among yard shrubs, in cattle shelters and in small dugouts. Most such animals were found dead later.

According to moose biologist, Dr. Vince Crichton, mortality in Manitoba was extensive and concentrated in western regions such as Turtle, Duck, Riding, and Porcupine mountain areas. Hunters in these regions observed few

FIGURES 2.4 and 2.5. Hungry, cold, weak, irritable and tick-laden moose wander into acreages, farms and towns looking for shelter and easily available food. Some die. [LYLE FULLERTON].

moose in autumn 2002. Fall counts, 2002, of moose in Riding Mountain National Park were 80% to 90% below counts in 2001.

■ Other hosts

As with moose, most elk in western North America become infested with winter ticks each year of their life. The exact relationship between winter ticks and elk is not known, except to say that ticks cause fewer problems for elk than moose, probably because they host fewer ticks. Infestations of winter ticks on elk may cause morbidity and mortality, but no critical studies have been done. Nonetheless, strong statements appear in early literature. A 1917 paper by C. W. Howard reported that elk imported from Montana to Minnesota and released in a state park were "heavily infested" with winter ticks for several years. In his classic text *The Elk of North America*, published in 1951, Olaus Murie stated that "...the winter tick is a never-failing scourge that visits the elk each spring, its numbers varying from year to year". John Stelfox, a well-known wildlife biologist, formerly with the Canadian Wildlife Service, agreed, stating (1962) that winter ticks were the proximal cause of death during severe winters in the 1960s "...when the animal's condition is greatly impaired by diminishing food supplies, increased energy losses required to combat deep snow and cold weather".

Most domestic animals escape problems from winter ticks, but horses and cattle can suffer from infestation. A 1913 paper by Bishop and Wood stated that adult horses in California, Montana and Oregon became weak, and some colts died if not treated promptly for winter tick infestation. A 1927 paper from British Columbia by E. A. Bruce stated that winter ticks caused anemia and death in horses in the Okanagan area. Cameron and Fulton (1926-1927) reported serious losses of cattle and horses in areas frequented by moose where settlers were "carving homesteads from the virgin forests" in Saskatchewan. In Alberta, there are few reports of horses and cattle infested with winter ticks, and those occur in winters when tick numbers on moose are high. Given the number of horses on acreages around Edmonton, where moose and winter ticks are numerous, one would expect high exposure of horses to winter ticks. Yet, reports are rare.

Most domestic animals escape problems from winter ticks, but horses and cattle can suffer from infestation.

All moose in Alberta become infested with winter ticks every year of their life.

The life of a winter tick

■ What makes winter ticks *tick*?

Winter ticks have one idiosyncrasy that sets them apart from all other ticks in Canada: they complete their entire life cycle on one animal. They are a one-host tick (FIGURE 3.1).

All ticks have three parasitic life stages—the larva, nymph and adult—all of which require a meal of blood, which they get from feeding on a vertebrate host, and which they need to moult to the next life stage. Most ticks use different hosts for the larval, nymphal and adult life stage, but not the winter ticks. All three blood-feeding stages of winter ticks feed from the same

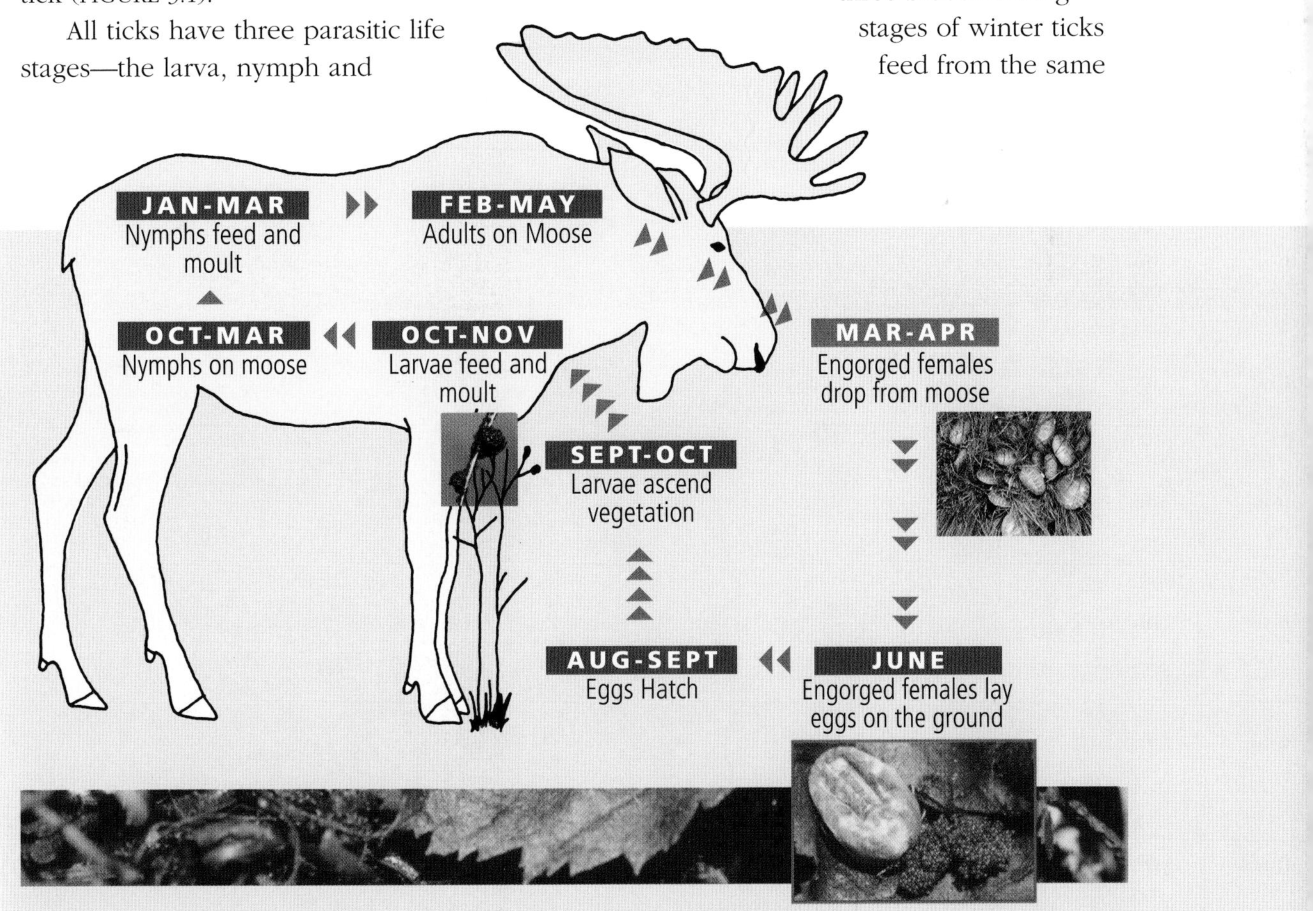

JAN-MAR
Nymphs feed and moult

FEB-MAY
Adults on Moose

OCT-MAR
Nymphs on moose

OCT-NOV
Larvae feed and moult

MAR-APR
Engorged females drop from moose

SEPT-OCT
Larvae ascend vegetation

AUG-SEPT
Eggs Hatch

JUNE
Engorged females lay eggs on the ground

FIGURE 3.1. Life cycle of winter ticks on moose. Winter ticks are one-host ticks, which means that all life stages that require a meal of blood—larvae, nymphs and adults—feed from the same host individual.

host individual. Thus, each and every tick on an infested moose, elk or deer takes three separate blood meals, once as a larva, once as a nymph, and once as an adult, all on the same animal over winter.

In addition, the northern yearly cycle of winter ticks follows a precise pattern that varies little from year to year. The timing of a winter tick's finding a host, feeding on that host, dropping from that host and laying eggs in the duff layer, follows a predictable and non-varying annual pattern. The probable reason why winter ticks must be so precise in the timing of their life cycle is that, as ticks go, the north is a cold place to live; they barely have enough time to complete their cycle so far north. As will be shown later, if winter ticks make any mistakes in getting from host-to-host, cold will get them. As a result, year in and year out, a winter tick's life in Alberta is virtually unchanged. That is what makes them tick, so to speak: doing the same things at the same time every year.

Winter ticks begin their life in the spring as eggs. This occurs when adult female ticks that have fed on host blood and have mated with males, drop from moose or another large mammal and move into the duff litter where they lay eggs in late May and early June. Each female tick produces several thousand eggs, then dies.

In late summer, eggs hatch to sand granule-sized larvae, often called seed ticks. Larvae are less than 1 millimetre long (approximately $^1/_{32}$ inch) and have three pairs of walking legs.

Larvae climb grasses, shrubs and small trees and form aggregations (FIGURE 3.2) from late August to mid-October (see Drew and Samuel, 1985). There they wait to ambush a moose.

It is not known what activates winter tick larvae to climb vegetation and form clumps. Factors suggested include the advent of frost, decreasing day length or decreasing soil

FIGURE 3.2. Larval winter ticks climb vegetation in late summer and early autumn, form clumps and ambush moose. [PERMISSION FROM ALCES AND ELSEVIER].

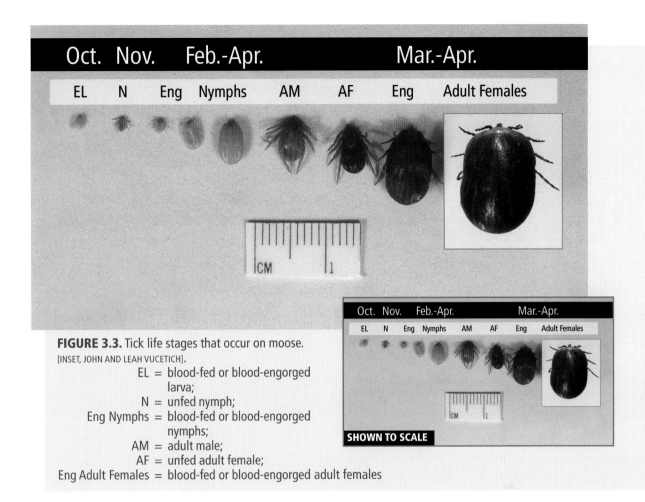

FIGURE 3.3. Tick life stages that occur on moose.
[INSET, JOHN AND LEAH VUCETICH].

EL = blood-fed or blood-engorged larva;
N = unfed nymph;
Eng Nymphs = blood-fed or blood-engorged nymphs;
AM = adult male;
AF = unfed adult female;
Eng Adult Females = blood-fed or blood-engorged adult females

temperature. Decreasing day length in autumn might be the major factor that cues larvae to climb because of its year-to-year constancy.

Once on vegetation, seed ticks wait in ambush (tick biologists call this "questing") for moose, elk, deer and other large mammals to pass and come in contact with the clump. Hosts become infested from September to early November when, during the course of feeding on, and moving through vegetation, they contact a clump of tick larvae. Peak numbers of aggregating larvae occur in late September and early October. This coincides with an active period for moose, the breeding season.

During the breeding season, moose, especially males, are constantly on the move, a behaviour that places them at risk of infestation.

Larvae that do not attach to a host in the short period of time between climbing vegetation in August and September and the first extended period of cold weather, which usually occurs by mid-November, die. None survives winter.

Once on moose, larvae feed on blood, and by November they moult to the nymphal life stage (FIGURE 3.3), which is about 1.7 millimetres long (about $\frac{1}{16}$ inch) with four pairs of legs. Nymphs are dormant on moose for several months (FIGURE 3.4). They begin

Summary of the predictable times for the various life stages of winter ticks in Alberta.

Late May-early June	Female tick lays eggs on ground. Then she dies. Moose are tick-free.
Late summer	Eggs hatch to sand granule-sized larvae. Moose are tick-free.
Late August to mid-October	Larvae climb vegetation and form clumps.
September to early November	Larvae ambush and attach to moose, elk, deer and other large mammals, but not humans. Those larvae that do not find a host die.
By November	Larvae on moose have fed on blood and moult to the nymphal life stage.
November to late January	Unfed nymphs remain dormant on moose.
Late January through March	Nymphs feed on blood and moult to adult ticks.
Late March, April, early May	Both sexes of adult ticks feed on blood, mate on the host, then drop from moose, females first.

Development of Winter Ticks

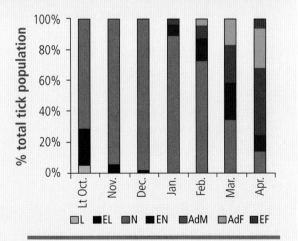

FIGURE 3.4. Developmental chronology of winter ticks on moose beginning in late October with larvae (L) that have just attacked moose from vegetation, and moving through autumn, winter and spring as blood-fed or engorged larvae (EL), nymphs (N), blood-fed or engorged nymphs (EN), adult males (AdM), adult females (AdF), and blood-fed or engorged adult females (EF).

taking blood meals in late January and moult to the adult stage in February and March. Peak numbers of blood-fed nymphs occur on moose in mid-February.

Adult female winter ticks are dark, reddish-brown, about 6.5 millimetres long (¼ inch), with four pairs of legs and no pattern on their back. Adult male winter ticks are similar, except they have a white crosshatch pattern on their dark brown back. During March and April both sexes feed on blood and mate on the host. Males take little blood, only enough to provide the energy to produce sperm. They spend most of their time searching for females with which to mate. Females, on the other hand, take a large blood meal so as to produce as many eggs as possible. Females of the Rocky Mountain wood tick, *Dermacentor andersoni*, feed on blood before, during and after copulation; presumably, winter ticks do the same. Blood-engorged females may reach 1.5 centimetres (⅝ inch) in length.

After dropping from moose, female ticks move to the soil surface, preferably under a layer of leaves, where they lay their eggs in sheltered places. Then they die and the cycle is complete. Male ticks remain on moose, deer and elk a while longer searching for female ticks, but by about mid-May, animals have few if any ticks. The tick attack is over, at least for this year.

In summary, there is one generation of ticks per year in Alberta and other northern areas. Ticks parasitize moose and other vertebrate hosts from September and October until April and early May. Animals are tick-free over summer.

As indicated, winter ticks in Alberta have a very seasonal and predictable life cycle that varies little from year-to-year. This trait was used in a legal case in which an Alberta man was charged with illegal possession of wild game (moose) out of season. The story, which appeared in the Athabasca, Alberta newspaper *The Echo*, November 10, 1982, then later in scientific publication (Samuel, 1988), follows.

Fish and Wildlife officers searched a premises acting on a tip that a moose had been poached in March. Bits of hair and small pieces of hide were found near some outbuildings. The officers collected and brought those pieces of hide to our research laboratory. No background information was provided regarding the case, not even that poaching was suspected. We were merely asked to provide information on date of death.

In court, a forensic scientist testified that the hair and bits of tissue found on the premises of the accused were those of moose. However, he could not tell when the animal had been killed. The accused admitted the pieces of hide were from a moose he killed, but claimed he had killed the moose during the November hunting season. Based on the known life cycle of winter tick, for that claim to be true, almost 100% of the ticks would have been in the unfed nymph stage,[12] because, as shown in Figure 3.4, close to 100% of ticks found on moose from November until late January are unfed nymphs.

About 900 ticks were recovered from the pieces of hide. Only 26% were unfed nymphs, another 28% were fed nymphs and 46% were adult ticks. Based on these data, we testified that the moose did not die in November, but was shot after February, probably in late March or early April. The defendant was found guilty as charged and fined the maximum amount. Score one for the good guys.

In summary, there is one generation of ticks per year in Alberta and other northern areas. Ticks parasitize moose and other vertebrate hosts from September and October until April and early May.

---

[12] "Unfed" means that the nymphal tick life-stage had not yet fed on blood.

Tick larvae climb and form clumps on vegetation at heights of their preferred large mammalian hosts.

How ticks are adapted to attacking moose

In nature, ticks find hosts in one of two ways: hunting and ambushing. Hunter ticks actively move to their host; ambushers passively lie in wait for an approaching host, a s-*tick*-up, so to speak. Winter ticks are ambushers, which means that the young seed ticks (larvae) position themselves on tall grasses, shrubs and small trees in autumn and wait for hosts to pass nearby. When hosts get close enough, bingo, they get ambushed.

> "The war general is skillful in attack whose opponent does not know what to defend..."
>
> FROM 'THE ART OF WAR' BY SUN TZU...ABOUT 500 B.C.

◼ Tick tac-*ticks*

Winter tick larvae have several characteristics that appear to be adaptive for increasing the likelihood of contacting a large mammalian host in autumn. These adaptations appear to be particularly important in moose country where the period of ambush is short, because autumn is short and winter is long. A tick cannot attack a host when frozen! Proposed adaptations are:

▪ Be *sense*-ible

Ticks have receptor "sense" organs near the ends of their first pair of legs that aid in recognizing the approach of suitable hosts. Ticks become active in response to a variety of factors including carbon dioxide in the breath of approaching hosts, shade produced by a nearby host, even vibration from a large host walking nearby. Some ticks can detect carbon dioxide at more than 20 metres. We often blow on clumps of ticks in the field in cold weather to determine how long it takes them to become active.

Time from inactivity to activity is short when the weather is warm and increases to several minutes when it is cold. In September and October, when average daytime temperatures are usually above freezing, ticks respond to human breath in a second or two. By early November, when average temperatures are below freezing, response times increase to a minute or more indicating that a moose would literally have to be standing next to a clump for several minutes for the ticks to become active enough to hitch a ride.

▪ Form clumps

The primary reason for young ticks aggregating in clumps on

FIGURE 4.1. Young ticks moving from vegetation to host (a finger, at left, serves as the host in this case). Legs of larvae in clumps appear interlocked. When one larva contacts the finger, a string of larvae is "pulled" from the clump to the host. [RANDY MANDRYK]

vegetation must be to improve the odds of attacking a host such as moose. Other species of ticks ascend vegetation only when the known host is most active; for example, a deer at dawn and dusk. At other times the ticks descend to ground level to replenish water. Young winter ticks do not do that, but rather ascend vegetation once, form clumps and remain there until a host is found or they are buried by snow, blown off, or die.

Maybe the clump itself is an adaptation to prevent the ticks from becoming desiccated.

But, forming clumps is certainly a way for many ticks to attach to moose at one time. This happens because these young ticks are also…

■ **Acro-ba-*ticks***

Legs of larvae in clumps appear interlocked (FIGURE 4.1). In other words, when a moose, elk or deer approaches, the larvae at the surface of the clump wave their front legs hoping to touch and grab onto the animal (questing). At the same time, the hind legs appear interlocked with larvae in the middle of the clump. Thus, upon touching a host, the larvae on the surface of the clump literally drag many larvae to the host!

Another adaptation, never before mentioned by anyone to my knowledge, I call "coin-flipping" or the "tiddlywinks" flip. Several years ago, one of my students was seated at a microscope observing a clump of active ticks and excitedly claimed that they were jumping. I calmly reminded her that fleas jump, not ticks. The student responded that she knew that, but "these ticks look to me like they are jumping".

Indeed, she was correct. Bathed in a sea of carbon dioxide from human or moose breath, clumps of larvae become very active. And in the midst of this activity, the odd tick larva, sometimes with another tick on its back, will suddenly flip end over end, landing several millimetres from the launch site. This is obviously done in hopes of landing on the hair coat of the nearby moose, elk or deer.

We also see what I call the "droplet drop", where, in the midst of clump activity, a smaller clump at the surface of the main clump will form in a teardrop that drops from the main clump. This is obviously done in hopes of landing on the passing host.

■ Form clumps at the right height

One might think that ticks would merely climb vegetation and form aggregations or clumps at random. They do not! Rather, they climb, then cease climbing and form clumps at or near tips of vegetation at heights of their preferred large mammal hosts. Michelle McPherson, an undergraduate student in my laboratory, released larvae at the base of simulated vegetation (tall nylon rods), then measured the heights of clumped larvae 24 hours later (see McPherson and co-authors, 2000).

To our amazement, larvae climbed to the height of the body of deer, elk and moose. Mean height of formed clumps of larvae was 125 centimetres (FIGURE 4.2 and 4.3). Few settled on the rods below 50 centimetres, probably because in the wild that would place them in the leg region of the host animals, and they would be brushed off a leg easily as the host moved through the vegetation. Also, few clumps formed above the body height of their intended hosts.

We recently repeated this same experiment using winter ticks from Oklahoma where the main hosts are deer and cattle. Of course, cattle do not stand nearly as tall as moose; the shoulder height of an adult cow is approximately 110 centimetres. Mean height of clumps was only 77 centimetres. This suggests that winter ticks are adapted to heights of regionally preferred hosts: in Alberta they range from deer to moose and, in Oklahoma, from deer to cattle.

■ Form clumps at the right time

Breeding time is a time of great activity among wild big game. Males (bulls and bucks), in particular, spend most waking hours in breeding activities such as scent marking, tending females (cows and does), fighting other males, etc. In so doing, they cover a lot of ground and, incidentally, rub against a lot of bush.

In Alberta, elk breed from early to late September, moose from late September to mid-October and deer in November. And when are winter tick larvae most numerous on vegetation? You guessed it, from late September through early November. Peak numbers occur in early-to-mid

October, during the moose rut, but after the elk rut and before deer become active. This might be one of the reasons why elk and deer have fewer winter ticks than moose.

The length of time tick clumps are on vegetation, waiting for a moose or other large mammal to pass close by, can be as long as 3½ months in years of mild weather (that is, early September to mid-December) and as short as 1½ months, when winter arrives early. Meteorological factors such as cold, wind and snow affect numbers and activity of larvae on vegetation. Wind scatters larvae, snow buries larvae, and cold inactivates larvae. For example, a major snowstorm in mid-October, 1991, accompanied by unseasonably cold weather, virtually ended the transmission season for that year in central Alberta. The area received approximately 40 centimetres of snow and temperature lows were below minus 15° Celsius for several weeks. Most larvae were buried by snow and the transmission period that year was essentially cut in half.

- ### Form clumps at the right orientation

Once on vegetation, winter tick larvae display a number of orientation responses that increase their survival, thus aiding in finding a host. They clump on the shady leeward side

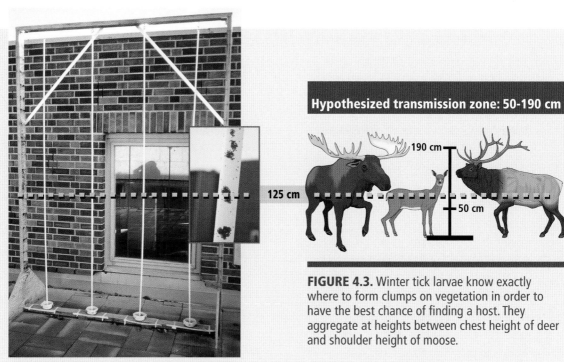

FIGURE 4.3. Winter tick larvae know exactly where to form clumps on vegetation in order to have the best chance of finding a host. They aggregate at heights between chest height of deer and shoulder height of moose.

FIGURE 4.2. Nylon rods were used to simulate vegetation in an experiment to determine whether or not tick larvae climbed to the body height of their preferred hosts. Indeed, 80% of 400 clumps formed (inset) at heights above ground between 50 centimetres (that is, chest height of deer) and 190 centimetres (shoulder height of moose). Mean height of tick clumps was 125 centimetres. In other words, winter ticks climb vegetation to the height of the hosts to which they want to attach.

FIGURE 4.4. The photograph illustrates the difficulty female ticks have in moving once they drop from moose to lay their eggs. Basically, near where they hit the ground is where they must lay their eggs. [JOHN AND LEAH VUCETICH].

of vegetation, probably to avoid the desiccating effects of sun or being dislodged by wind.

Not everyone agrees that heat from sunlight causes dehydration in ticks, but we found that, on sunny days, larval clumps shifted their position slightly to avoid being in direct sun. They did not change their vertical height above ground, just moved to get out of the sun.

Regarding wind, the strongest winds in autumn in central Alberta generally blow from the northwest and average over 20 kilometres per hour, while the most persistent (but milder) winds blow from the south. Most clumps of larvae form on the easterly side of natural vegetation.

■ Odds and ends

It would be interesting if young ticks had a preference for climbing the plants that moose prefer to eat; that would be quite an adaptation. But we have no evidence this occurs. What we know is that the female ticks that drop from moose in March and April to lay their eggs have short legs relative to their huge blood-filled body (FIGURE 4.4). Because of this, they have difficulty walking great distances. Picture the fattest mouse imaginable with its small short legs. For that mouse to move would involve a rocking chair motion of its body because it would be so fat that its feet could not all touch the ground at the same time. Same idea holds for blood-filled winter ticks. The large pea- to small grape-sized organism with its four pairs of short legs sticking out to the side has difficulty moving through the vegetation.

We confirmed that where female ticks drop is essentially where they will lay their eggs. And this indicates that where moose spend their time in March and April is where the female must lay her eggs and where those eggs must develop to young ticks that will climb vegetation and attack moose in autumn. If it is a grassy meadow, then larvae will ascend grass in autumn. If it is along a moose trail in aspen-shrub habitat, then larvae will ascend small aspen and shrubs. If the habitat is suitable for tick survival and development, then a good crop of tick larvae will be found on vegetation the following autumn.

Sounds a little reckless, but the process must work because we have data (see Chapter 5) that indicate that most, if not all, moose, elk and deer in central Alberta, likely elsewhere, become infested with winter ticks every year.

In what vegetative habitats are moose when female ticks drop from them in March and April? Oscar Aalangdong, one of my graduate students, studied these questions in Elk Island National Park (Aalangdong, 1994). He sampled the numbers of tick larvae on various types of vegetation by dragging white flannel sheets through various habitats in autumn. He found that most tick larvae were in aspen forest and habitats dominated by shrubs. These were habitats with relatively sparse tree canopies. Summer temperatures in these areas are several degrees higher than in habitats such as spruce forest with dense canopies. Ticks in more open areas survived better and were more productive than those in dense canopy habitats such as spruce forest.

Aalangdong's research was done in the early 1990s, when upland aspen habitats—most with open canopies, some less so—made up about 60% of Elk Island Park. He put female ticks in these habitats and found that over 70% survived to lay eggs, which hatched to become an average of over 600 larvae from each female tick. Norm Cool, researcher at the Park, determined that almost two-thirds of moose seen in Elk Island Park were in or near aspen-dominated forest. In Alberta, aspen habitats appear to be good habitats for both winter ticks and moose.

This probably explains why moose that live in areas of Alberta with relatively open canopies—those aspen-dominated areas between the prairies and boreal forest of central Alberta, and areas near the Peace River in northwestern Alberta—appear to suffer more from winter ticks than moose living in spruce-dominated, boreal-mixedwood forests. Because ticks survive best in the open-canopied areas dominated by aspen, poplar, grasses and shrubs, moose in these areas probably acquire more ticks than they do in spruce-dominated forests. The reality is that the forest floor of spruce forests is likely too cold in summer for eggs to hatch to larvae in large numbers.

One remaining question, in the face of these extraordinary adaptations of winter ticks to contact a moose, elk or deer, is to discover how successful they are in their quest. One barometer of success is how many animals are infested annually. We have found that most, if not all, deer, elk and moose in Alberta become infested with winter ticks each autumn of their lives. How many larvae they acquire is not certain, but we have estimated that about 8% of larvae that establish on a host in autumn survive to become mature adult female ticks in late winter on moose. We know that, on average, moose in late winter host around 30,000 ticks, indicating they likely acquire several hundred thousand larvae in autumn.

Are these estimates reasonable? Yes, they are. We once examined a captive 2½-year-old male reindeer that died in November at the Valley Zoo in Edmonton. The animal, housed outdoors next to a group of moose that were presumably infested with ticks, had an estimated 411,661 winter ticks. This is 24 ticks per square centimetre body surface, or 155 ticks per square inch! If there were a category in the *Guinness Book of World Records* for greatest number of ticks on one animal, this would surely be the winner. Seriously, these data tell us that animals can indeed acquire a huge number of winter tick larvae from vegetation in autumn.

In summary, the ambushing adaptations of winter tick larvae and the synchrony of larvae and moose activities play a major role in transmission of winter ticks from vegetation to moose. These adaptations appear to be particularly important in northern regions where the period of transmission is often shortened by the early arrival of winter.

In summary, the ambushing adaptations of winter tick larvae and the synchrony of larvae and moose activities play a major role in transmission of winter ticks from vegetation to moose.

Ticks can be so numerous on moose as to appear like shingles on a roof.

Number of ticks on moose:
Doing the Arithme-*tick*

How many winter ticks do large mammals acquire? For moose the answer can be so high as to be unbelievable. When we began our studies in the 1970s, we would "eyeball" an infested moose and guess that if the infestation was severe, the animal had several thousand ticks. Our estimates were way off, much too low. It soon became obvious that we needed a more quantitative survey technique, one that provided accurate, unbiased and comparable data for moose and other large mammals.

With tick numbers in the many thousands on moose, some rather unusual techniques must be used to determine exact numbers.

Graduate student Dwight Welch took on the task of developing a reliable yet time-saving technique for estimating tick numbers. The method Dwight chose involved using a solution of potassium hydroxide that dissolved the hair and skin, but did not dissolve the chitinous exoskeleton of ticks. Dissolving moose hides, or the hide of any large mammal, for ticks is a huge job. Thus, another goal was to determine the accuracy of sampling pieces of hide, rather than the whole hide, to estimate numbers of ticks. The technique (could be called a *tick*-nique!) is as follows:

- The moose hide is removed from a fresh carcass and split in half from nose to tail along the dorsal midline.
- The half hide is spread on a flat surface and scored, non-hair side up, into squares (10 centimetres to a side) using a carpenter's chalk line (FIGURE 5.1).
- The hide is sketched on graph paper to determine its surface area.
- Each 100-centimetre square of hide is numbered and put into a jar with heated potassium hydroxide into which is added a

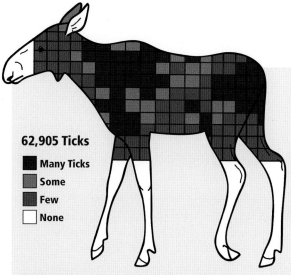

62,905 Ticks

■ Many Ticks
■ Some
■ Few
□ None

FIGURE 5.1. Moose hides were scored into squares.

small amount of liquid detergent to disperse aggregations of subcutaneous fat.

- When the hair and tissue, but not the ticks, are dissolved, the solution is passed through a small sieve to trap ticks.
- Sieved material is flushed with water into white pans and all ticks are counted for each piece of hide using a magnifying lens.

It takes several days to examine each half hide in this manner.

We collected data from 20 such moose hides (Welch and Samuel, 1989) and from this learned that a random sample of 15% of the half hide provides an accurate estimate of the total density of ticks on an animal; that is, the number of ticks per square centimetre of body surface. Total number of ticks can be predicted from tick density. Adopting this technique was a lot

of work, but many hours of labour were saved.

Armed with this time-saving procedure, we found average tick numbers of about 33,000 for 214 moose hides from western Canada. Two-thirds of the moose had 10,000 to 50,000 ticks and 19% had over 50,000 (FIGURE 5.2). Six percent had over 80,000 and 3% had more than 100,000 ticks.

To imagine how great these burdens would be on a moose, the density of ticks on a calf with 50,000 is 3.1 ticks per square centimetre body surface. For those of us still metrically challenged, this is an astonishing 20 ticks per square inch of body surface. The two most heavily infested moose, a bull with 150,000 ticks and a calf with 145,000 ticks, had densities of 5.7 and 7.8 ticks per square centimetre body surface, respectively, or 37 and 50 ticks per square inch, respectively (FIGURE 5.3).

Other hosts such as elk, deer and bison have far fewer ticks. In Elk Island National Park, near Edmonton, moose average about 37,000 ticks over winter (TABLE 5.1). This is about 30 times more winter ticks than are found on elk, 70 times more than deer and 280 times more than bison. Densities of ticks on moose are 28 and 32 times more than that on elk and deer, respectively, and 184 times more than on bison.

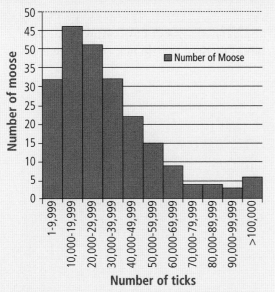

Frequency Distribution of Ticks on Moose

FIGURE 5.2. Few moose are overwhelmed with ticks though numbers of ticks are high. Few have over 100,000 ticks, but almost 20% host over 50,000 ticks.

TABLE 5.1. Average numbers of ticks and tick densities on moose, elk, deer and bison from Elk Island National Park, central Alberta.
[DATA COLLECTED BETWEEN 1978 AND 1990 AND REPORTED IN MOORING AND SAMUEL, 1998b].

Species	Ticks per animal	Ticks per cm² skin
Moose	37,070	1.660
Elk	1,200	0.059
White-tailed Deer	540	0.053
Bison	133	0.009

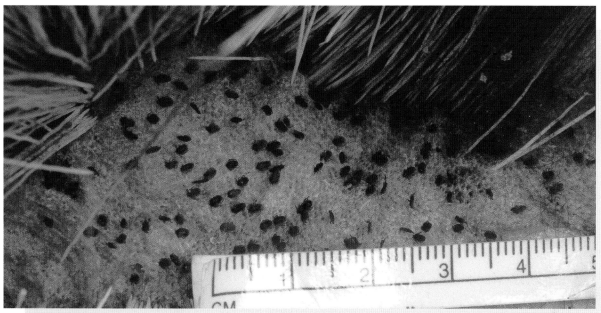

FIGURE 5.3. A poor but telling photograph showing high density of ticks on moose the year of a major tick-associated die-off of moose. This is the neck region of a hunter-killed moose. Cecil Cross and I found this moose hide under the snow while visiting a hunting campsite near Ft. Assiniboine, Alberta in April 1999. It was obviously from a kill made the previous November. Perhaps we can assume that this moose is indicative of tick numbers on moose in central Alberta that entered the winter of 1999.

All of several hundred moose we have examined in winter have been infested with winter ticks. All of 56 elk hides from Elk Island and Jasper national parks, Alberta, and National Elk Refuge, Wyoming were infested. Eight of 10 white-tailed deer, and 7 of 8 bison, from Elk Island Park were infested.

It is assumed that if tick numbers are sufficient there will be an energy cost, a drain to moose. If the drain is high, host animals are weakened and become more vulnerable to predation and disease, less able to compete with other animals for food, and less able to provide an ample supply of milk to young calves.

The cost of hosting ticks is usually divided into several categories: vectoring diseases, blood loss, effect on host survival and reproduction, and altered host behaviour. Although it is difficult to collect good data for wildlife, the cost of tick infestation has been well documented for cattle. Studies (summarized in Mooring and Samuel, 1998c) have shown that one blood-feeding female tick (not the winter tick, but another species of tick) can deprive a growing calf of up to 3.1 kilograms in weight-gain for that year and, if the calf has a moderate tick load, up to 44 kilograms in deprived growth. Reasons for this are clear: ticks consume blood, and toxins in their salivary gland secretions, which are introduced during tick feeding, depress appetite.

The cost to moose with winter ticks has not been documented with much precision, but an attempt to do so is made in the next chapter.

Close-up view of the skin of a moose that has removed much of its winter hair coat during grooming for ticks (see the attached adult male tick that survived the grooming process in the centre of the picture). What remains is skin with a thick, leathery appearance, first wet, but now with dry lesions crusted with dried blood.

Invasive characteristics of winter ticks for moose

We tend to think of wildlife as generally being healthy, which they are. We also tend to think that larger animals are more resilient when it comes to the battle they wage with diseases and parasites. Given that moose weigh up to 650 kilograms, or 1400 pounds, shouldn't they be able to handle 50,000 ticks or more with ease? Maybe not.

The general categories of problems that have been documented for winter ticks on moose are:

1. anemia from blood loss, and other physiological effects;
2. damage to and loss of the winter coat of hair, the result of the moose grooming ticks;
3. reduced stores of visceral fat;
4. decreased time spent feeding by moose as grooming time increases;
5. restlessness;
6. reduced growth in young moose.

These problems are summarized here.

■ (1) Anemia and other physiological effects

Ticks suck

Ticks are well adapted to feed on blood. Their complicated mouthparts are adapted for ripping and tearing at skin and the blood vessels it contains. The result is lesions at the base of the outer layer of skin, the epidermis, and into the inner layer, the dermis, where the blood vessels are found. Winter ticks cut the skin using a pair of serrated mouthparts called chelicerae. They then insert a toothed tube, the hypostome, which draws the blood (FIGURE 6.1).

Winter ticks have short mouthparts. In order to resist being dislodged by grooming, their salivary glands secrete a tough, rubbery cement, which seals the lesion and holds the feeding tick in place.

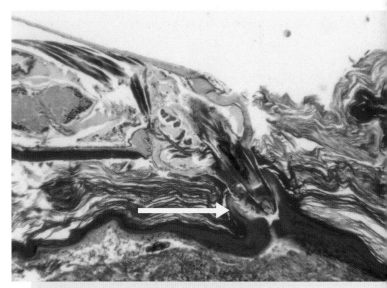

FIGURE 6.1. Cross-section of feeding winter tick showing backward-directed projections (arrow). The projections are part of a rod-shaped tube called the hypostome; it draws the blood. They, along with a tough rubbery cement (dark pink colour below the hypostome) secreted by the tick, seal the wound and hold the tick in place while feeding. [JOHN SUGIMOTO, COLORADO DIVISION OF WILDLIFE].

Ticks in general are voracious but sloppy feeders; that is, they create pools of blood from which they suck blood and other fluids that drain into the wound and also inject salivary gland secretions at the same time. Once attached, they feed slowly for several days. As blood is drawn in, various chemicals in a watery solution of saliva are secreted into the host. These chemicals permit the tick to stay attached by anesthetizing the bite area, thus avoiding detection, depressing coagulation, reducing inflammation and suppressing the immune response.

One finding that remained unexplained for years stemmed from the observation of what appeared to be much dried blood associated with blood-engorging female winter ticks on moose in March and April. Following discussion with Dr. Reuben Kaufman, tick physiologist at the University of Alberta, I am convinced that this is undigested hemoglobin. Kaufman (1971) and others have shown that much of the ingested blood meal of a close relative of the winter tick, the Rocky Mountain wood tick *Dermacentor andersoni*, fed on domestic rabbits, is passed in the feces as virtually unchanged hemoglobin (the oxygen-carrying protein pigment in the red blood cells). If winter ticks do this, which seems to be the case, they are feeding on a lot of blood that passes through them unchanged (FIGURE 6.2). I am not sure what this means for the tick, but moose lose in the equation, as you will see in the following discussion.

There are two widely diverging potential outcomes of this interaction. Perhaps, because moose are large and ticks are small (even the largest life stage, the blood-fed adult female, weighs a maximum of only about 0.8 gram), the burden of hosting 30,000, 50,000, or 80,000 ticks is not great. Then again, ticks in large numbers on any host should cause anemia, which could be serious or lethal.

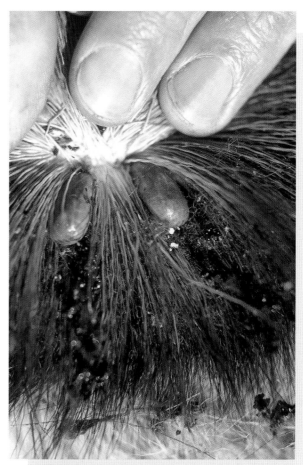

FIGURE 6.2. Blood-feeding female winter ticks appear to consume far more blood than they can use, because there is much dried blood in their feces. This is obvious in this picture of two blood-engorged, adult, female winter ticks. This blood could well be a source of the blood-stains seen in the snow along moose tracks and in moose beds in March and April (see Figure 2.1).

Anemia is the reduction below normal of either the red blood cells, or the quantity of hemoglobin, or both. It occurs when the equilibrium between blood loss and blood production is disturbed, as by feeding ticks.

One way to put high numbers of ticks in a blood-loss perspective is to estimate the amount of blood consumed. That is easier said than done.

It would appear intuitive that one could calculate the amount of blood consumed by ticks by simply weighing them before and after they feed. It is not that simple because feeding by ticks is a complicated process. Ticks do not simply take in blood during feeding. They concentrate the diluted blood meal to the essential nutrients by using their salivary glands to pump much of the watery wastes of the meal back into the host's circulation. And, as mentioned above, winter ticks appear to pass moose blood through their system undigested. So, unfortunately, the weight of the blood-fed tick is not an accurate representation of the amount of blood consumed. In fact, ticks may consume or process two-to-three times as much blood as their body weight after feeding.

Researchers (e.g., Koch and Sauer, 1984) have used a variety of analyses to estimate blood loss to ticks. The estimates of consumption by one female tick (of various species) range from 0.6 to 8.8 millilitres of blood. Kaufman and Phillips (1973) estimated consumption of about 4 millilitres of blood for the Rocky Mountain wood tick (*Dermacentor andersoni*). With these kinds of ranges in blood consumption by ticks, let's see if we can make a rough calculation of the amount of blood moose lose to winter ticks.

Taking a simplistic, and somewhat conservative, approach throughout this calculation, adult male ticks are removed from the blood-loss equation because they consume little blood, only enough to energetically provide for producing sperm. Also, the blood loss from the other blood-feeding stages on moose—the larvae and nymphs—will be ignored, even though blood loss to feeding nymphs might be considerable (go back and have another look at the picture of engorged nymphs in Figure 3.3). Finally, rather than suggest that winter tick females consume 4 millilitres of blood, as indicated for the Rocky Mountain

wood tick, or that they consume three times their blood-fed weight, as indicated in some tick literature, the figure used here will be twice their blood-fed weight. This is a bit conservative, but let's see where this takes us.

What is the blood-fed weight of an adult female winter tick? Addison and colleagues (1998a) found that engorged female winter ticks weighed more than 0.8 grams, while former graduate student Vicky Glines (1983) recorded a mean weight of 0.61 grams for fed-females. To be conservative, the latter figure was considered for use.[13]

How much blood does a moose have to lose? There are no data, so we must extrapolate from other animals. Blood volume for horses is estimated to be 8% to 10% of their body weight. Cameron and Luick (1972) estimated seasonal changes in blood volume of reindeer from about 6% to 9% of their body weight. Again, though one could go with 6%, estimates for moose will be based on 8% body weight—for the sake of being as accurate as possible, and relatively conservative.

Fifteen bull moose in central Alberta, examined between 1977 and 1990, hosted a median 19,714 ticks in March and April. Of that number, 27.6%, or 5441, were adult females. Assuming that all female ticks survived and consumed or processed 1.00 millilitres of blood, which is twice their weight after feeding on blood, bulls lost an estimated minimum of 5.4 litres of blood in March and April. An average Alberta bull weighs approximately 400 kilograms at winter's end and has, using the 8% value, an estimated 32 litres of blood. Thus, bulls must replace an estimated minimum 16.9% of their blood volume in March and April.

---

[13] Drew and Samuel (1989) noted that the weight of engorged female ticks dropping from grooming moose, decreased gradually from early March to the end of April. Tick weights rose significantly in a moose that was sickly, and did not groom. Since most, or all, tick-infested moose groom in the wild, to account for the gradually dropping weights of ticks, we chose a more conservative weight to use in the analysis, 0.50 grams. (See Appendix at the end of the book for details of calculations.)

How about cows? Seventeen cow moose in central Alberta, examined between 1982 and 1989, had a median of 17,560 ticks in March and April. Eighteen percent, or 3161 ticks, were adult females. Assuming that each female tick consumed or processed 1.00 millilitres of blood, cows lost 3.2 litres of blood in March and April. Cows weigh about 360 kilograms at winter's end. Thus, they average about 29 litres of blood using the 8% figure for blood volume. Cows must replace an estimated minimum 11% of their blood volume during late winter and early spring. And this happens when most are in the last trimester of pregnancy. In a sense there are two parasites working energetically against the cow: her fetus and winter ticks.

The median number of winter ticks in March and April on twelve calves from central Alberta, examined between 1982 and 1990, was 31,731 ticks.[14] Perhaps they are more heavily infested than older moose because they have a much higher ratio of body surface to body volume. They would also lack the resistance to ticks that older moose might acquire through repeated annual infestations of winter ticks. Whatever the case, 8123 (25.6%) of those ticks were adult females. Calves weigh only about 175 kilograms at winter's end; blood volume is an estimated 14 litres using the 8% body weight figure. With 1.00 millilitres of blood loss for each female tick, calves lost an estimated 8.1 litres of blood, indicating that they must replace an estimated 57.9% their blood volume.

There is no argument that these estimates are crude; they might be way off the mark. But, even if blood loss estimates for calves were overestimated by 10%, 20%, or even 30%, the information is still worth

considering, because the blood loss is still high. Obviously, in some years tick numbers and resulting blood loss will be much less, but in other years tick numbers will be higher, and resulting blood loss will be greater. More research in this area is needed. For example, it must take a fair amount of energy for moose calves to replace the blood lost to ticks.

When moose die-offs occur, calves often make up a large proportion of the deaths. Anemia, caused by winter ticks, must be one of the major contributing factors. In fact, blood loss at these projected levels for calves should impact their ability to maintain an adequate plane of nutrition, considering that in March and April moose are already eating diets with marginal amounts of protein. Remember that calves are still growing during their first winter, and they must maintain an adequate blood energy level for growth and maintenance (heat production, for example). This is why calves rarely have fat stores by late December. Winter ticks are a major catalyst to the downward spiral of moose condition over winter.

For all moose, but most certainly for calves, ticks suck.

Blood loss is only one physiologic problem for moose. We found that well-fed captive moose experimentally infested with 30,000 larval-stage winter ticks in autumn later showed chronic weight loss, low albumen (important protein) content and decreased phosphates in the blood, along with transitory anemia, grooming and characteristic hair damage/loss. Decreased albumen is a nonspecific clinical change, common to a variety of conditions. It might simply reflect the stress associated with moose having lots of

---

[14] Some might say this value is inflated because calves are often found dead and such individuals likely have higher numbers of ticks than other moose. In reality, it is the opposite because many engorged females have already dropped from moose by mid- to late April, and two of the twelve calves died after April 15. If these two moose are deleted from the sample, the median rises to 43,784. If this figure is used, calves must replace 80% of their blood volume.

ticks, but it has been shown that other species of ticks can alter the synthesis of albumen. In another study using well-fed captive moose experimentally infested with 21,000 or 42,000 larval-stage winter ticks in autumn, Addison and colleagues (1998b) found that ticks had only limited impact on hematologic and biochemical parameters.

■ (2) Damage to, and loss of, the winter coat of hair, the result of moose grooming for ticks

Dras-*tick* measures: grooming those ticks

Moose groom for several reasons, such as conditioning the hair coat by removing dirt and excessive oil. But from late autumn through early spring, grooming is mainly in response to tick bite.

In order for a moose to groom, it must perceive the sensation of itch. John Alexander (1986) defined itch as "a curious sensation midway between pain and pleasure, which evokes an irresistible desire to scratch". He went on to differentiate pain from itch and pointed out that a pain stimulus will override and suppress an itch stimulus. This, of course, explains the benefit of severe scratching for stubborn itch.

When ticks feed on blood, there is a two-way exchange of fluids. Blood goes from moose to tick, and secretions from the tick's salivary gland are injected into the moose. These secretions contain pharmacologically active chemicals, which alert the immune system that something is amiss. Soon, granulocytic white blood cells collect at the bite site, releasing histamine. Histamine, a chemical involved in allergic reactions, causes inflammation, the body's response to injury, which leads to irritation, then itch at the bite site. Itch stimulates scratching or licking by moose, which is called grooming.

Moose use three modes of grooming to relieve the itch from biting ticks: oral grooming, scratching and rubbing (FIGURE 6.3). The tongue and lower front teeth (incisors and canines) are used in oral grooming. Such grooming is directed to the posterior part of the body, including chest, shoulder, foreleg, belly, flank, back, hind leg and rump. In some cases the

FIGURE 6.3. Moose grooming against winter ticks. Moose use three modes of grooming to relieve the itch from biting ticks: oral grooming, using mainly the tongue, scratching with hind hooves, and rubbing either against their own body (as in side of head or ears on lateral side of body) or woody vegetation. [FIGURES DRAWN BY EMMA MOORING, WITH PERMISSION OF ELSEVIER].

tongue is used alone, or the teeth and tongue are used in combination.

Scratching involves use of the rear hooves against the head, neck and mane and shoulder. Moose rub various parts of the body against solid, usually vertically oriented objects. Moose use trees and shrubs, or walk over downed or low vegetation and rub the sternum and groin. Alternatively, moose use the side of the head to rub against the side of the body (shoulder and flank). Two additional comfort behaviours, head shaking and body shaking, are performed separately or in conjunction with one of the other grooming behaviours.

Proof that grooming is solely aimed at eliminating winter ticks is based on a behavioural study (Samuel, 1991) of captive moose infested experimentally with winter ticks compared with captive moose with no ticks. In short, moose with ticks groomed, sometimes a lot; moose without ticks did not (FIGURE 6.4). Oral grooming, using the tongue and lower front teeth, and rubbing, were the two predominant behaviours observed for infested moose.

Hours Per Day Moose Spent Grooming

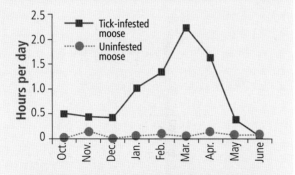

FIGURE 6.4. Shown here is the average time 13 captive moose, infested with winter ticks, and 11 captive moose, with no winter ticks, spent grooming. Time is extrapolated from many 15-minute observation periods made each month on each animal. Based on the information in this graph, it is obvious that in autumn, winter and spring, moose groom primarily in response to the irritation of biting ticks.

Grooming begins in late October, when the small larval seed ticks feed on blood and tissue fluids. By month, moose with ticks groom approximately ½ hour each day in late October, November and December, when a few larvae and nymphs are feeding on blood. At the same time, moose without ticks groom only a few seconds each day, sometimes not at all. Tick-infested moose groom an estimated 1 to 2⁺ hours each day from January to April, when the larger blood-feeding stages— nymphs and adults—are feeding. Moose without ticks seldom groom during this period, usually less than 10 seconds each hour. There is a major reduction in grooming by infested moose in May (22 minutes each day), when most ticks have dropped from moose, and in June (4 minutes each day), when moose are tick-free. Tick-free moose groom 4½ minutes each day in May and June. It is assumed that rubbing, which predominates then, is a response to the itching that accompanies annual replacement of winter hair with the summer coat of hair.

Of course, what is described here, for captive moose without ticks, never occurs in the wild, because we assume that virtually every moose in North America that lives south of 60° North latitude becomes infested annually with winter ticks.

Wild moose in Elk Island National Park spend just over an estimated hour each day grooming in March and April, the time of greatest annual stress for moose. The patterns of hair damage and loss, due to tick grooming by wild moose, are identical to patterns on captive moose experimentally infested with winter ticks.

Extent of damage to, and loss of, the winter coat of hair
Looking white as a ghost
When moose groom against ticks, they first roughen the hair, then break it off at

FIGURE 6.5. Progressive damage to the winter hair coat from grooming ticks. First, the hair coat is roughened (left). Then, the hair is broken to near its base, giving the moose a whitish or ghost look (centre). Some moose go beyond the ghost condition, in that the hair coat is almost completely destroyed from excessive grooming (right). The skin of these moose has a thickened leathery appearance, and is dark, dry and crusted with dried blood. Skin damage appears serious, but the summer coat is not affected, so there must be no permanent damage. [DWIGHT WELCH, LEFT; MIDDLE WITH PERMISSION OF ELSEVIER; JOHN AND LEAH VUCETICH (RIGHT)].

varying lengths. The well known "ghost moose" has broken hair over much of the body. In the worst case, the hair coat can be completely destroyed and the skin damaged (FIGURE 6.5).

Premature loss of the winter hair coat of moose is well documented. Sometimes damage and loss are slight, sometimes severe. Mooring and Samuel (1999) found that wild moose that groomed the most lost the most hair.[15] Hair damage and loss is most severe, hence most visible, in March and April.

Because most if not all moose in Alberta, likely elsewhere in southern Canada and northern United States, have ticks every year of their life, we might expect that most moose would groom against them and, hence, lose hair. And they do. During winter aerial and ground surveys, we found the following percentages of Alberta moose with hair loss from grooming against ticks: near the town of Rochester (98%); in the Swan Hills (68%); in Elk Island National Park (89%); and in Cypress Hills Interprovincial Park (60%) and Long Lake Provincial Park

(100%). We also observed moose in Manitoba's Riding Mountain National Park (100% with hair loss), near Jackson, Wyoming (32%) and Ogden, Utah (100%), and in Baxter State Park, Maine (100%).

The amount of grooming (expressed as hair loss) keeps pace with numbers of ticks so that it rises as numbers of ticks rise (FIGURE 6.6).

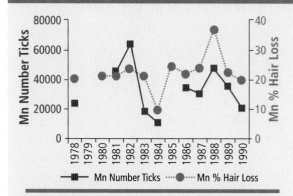

Average Yearly Hair Loss on Moose

Mn Number Ticks — Mn % Hair Loss

FIGURE 6.6. In general, average yearly amount of hair loss on moose (here termed "mean % hair loss") tends to keep pace with the average yearly number of ticks at Elk Island National Park. The assumption is that more ticks results in more grooming, and more grooming results in more hair loss.

---

[15] Loss of hair is called alopecia, which is the major clinical feature of moose infested with winter ticks.

FIGURE 6.7. Sequence of premature loss of winter hair on moose infested with winter ticks. Light damage (top), with a small percentage of winter hair lost or broken, first occurs on the neck and shoulders, usually in January. (This picture was taken in March; note the large number of ticks just under the "bald" area at the base of the neck.) Moderate damage (middle) with approximately 30% to 40% lost or damaged coat of hair. Severe damage (next to bottom), with up to 80% lost or damaged coat of hair. Ghost moose (bottom) show more than 80% hair coat damaged or destroyed.
[PARKS CANADA, ELK ISLAND NATIONAL PARK, TOP TWO; DWIGHT WELCH, NEXT TO BOTTOM; ROLF PETERSON, BOTTOM].

Using results from our experimental studies in Alberta and those of Addison and McLaughlin (1988) in Ontario, we know that moose with winter ticks show a predictable and never-changing progression and distribution of damage to the coat of hair. That pattern is basically the same for all ticky moose (FIGURE 6.7).

It is rare for hair damage and loss to be seen before mid- to late January, when hair breakage begins to appear on the neck and shoulders. By mid-March the area of hair damage or loss expands rapidly to include a somewhat triangular pattern of loss across the saddle and chest anterior to, but not including, the facial area. The long dark hair of the mane is destroyed, too, apparently by a "sawing" motion using the shank bone of the lower hind leg, or by scratching with hooves of the hind leg. The area of lateral body surface with damaged or lost hair increases rapidly through March, ranging from 40% to 70%. Ghost moose show hair damage and loss exceeding 80% of the lateral body surface.

In years of many ticks and dying moose, wildlife biologists, Fish and Wildlife officers, park personnel, and members of the public commonly report ghost moose. The triangular pattern of hair loss is first seen and reported in March and April, followed by reports of ghost moose in April and May. Moose take on the ghost appearance, with hair loss on the outer surface of the ears, bell, neck, shoulders, withers, ribs, sternum, flank, belly and around the anus. I would venture a guess that most rural Canadians in moose country know the expression, and have seen, ghost moose.

Moose do not grow a separate winter and summer coat of hair, but replace the old winter coat of hair with new winter hair that begins to appear in spring, and grows through the summer. Samuel and colleagues (1986) described the sequence of the winter moult in captive moose with no ticks and found that new hair, called the summer hair, first appeared as shiny, black, oily hair on the front part of the upper hind legs in late April to early May (FIGURE 6.8). Summer hair then appeared on the ventral surface of the moose and on the face. It quickly spread up the sides; by late June the entire moose appeared coal black.

Reference books describing moult of the winter hair coat of moose have confused the tick-induced sequence of hair loss—the neck, shoulders, behind the hump, etc.—with the moult pattern. This is easy to understand given that most, or all, moose in southern Canada become tick-infested each year of their life and remove hair by grooming. In other words, the observed moult of winter hair for moose is most often that which is caused by grooming against winter ticks.

Tick-infested moose can have the entire coat of summer hair by early May,

while tick-free moose do not have the entire coat of summer hair until late June.

The ghost appearance stems from the fact that each of the outer hairs—the guard hairs—of the winter hair coat of moose consists of alternating colour bands. The pattern is called "agouti" after the name of a South American rodent, the agouti, which has banded hair. The two pigments found in mammalian hair are melanin, which gives hair its black and brown colours, and xanthophyll, which gives it the reddish-brown shades. The tips tend to be black from the concentration of melanin, becoming dark brown with the addition of xanthophyll. But the lower $\frac{1}{2}$ to $\frac{2}{3}$ of the hair shaft tends to be whitish-grey. Thus, when the distal or outer part of the hair coat is destroyed or broken off during grooming, the proximal, greyish part of the hair remains. Hence, the ghost appearance.

From this progression, categories of tick-induced hair loss—mild or light, moderate, severe and ghost—were

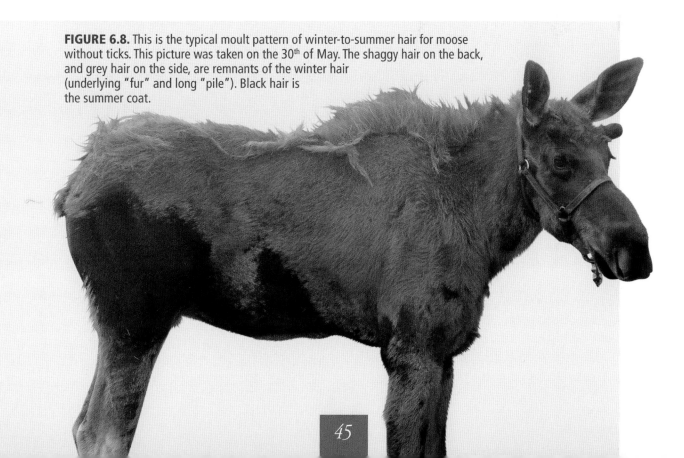

FIGURE 6.8. This is the typical moult pattern of winter-to-summer hair for moose without ticks. This picture was taken on the 30th of May. The shaggy hair on the back, and grey hair on the side, are remnants of the winter hair (underlying "fur" and long "pile"). Black hair is the summer coat.

developed for use by moose biologists during their winter aerial surveys (see Figure 6.7). Because most surveys of moose are done early in the year, when snow conditions provide a good background to observe and count moose, only the initial categories of hair loss are observed commonly. However, moose biologists can use the presence of tick-caused hair loss in early winter as a predictor of moose losses that might occur later that winter. In other words, if some ghost moose, or moose with moderate-to-severe hair damage, are seen in January, it suggests that tick numbers are high; there will be much hair loss in March and April and many ticky moose will die.

One can provide a bit more quantitative data for the assessment of damage to the pelage of moose caused by ticks, using photographs taken during aerial or ground surveys, or from diagrams of hair loss drawn on a moose silhouette diagram. In the laboratory, areas of the body exhibiting damaged hair are measured using a computer. The process involves a digitizer, which is like the mouse used with the computer, except that it has an attachment much like a scope on a rifle. Using the crosshairs of the attachment, the outline of the body surface areas with damaged or lost hair is drawn and the computer calculates the area. One can then compute the approximate percentage of total body surface damaged by grooming (see Figure 6.6).

The extent of tick problems can be compared for different moose populations using digitized data for hair damage and loss. For example, annual end-of-winter hair loss was extensive in a moose population near Rochester, Alberta (100 kilometres north of Edmonton), when compared with moose at Elk Island National Park, just east of Edmonton (FIGURE 6.9). That suggests that moose from the Rochester area had more ticks than did moose from Elk Island.

Cost-benefit summary of grooming for tick-infested moose

There are positive sides to grooming. Grooming brings some relief from the sensation of itch. At the same time, some ticks are removed before they have a chance to complete feeding on blood (see next chapter). But there are several negative sides, too, all related to the time and energy consumed by grooming.

1. Compulsive grooming is distracting; thus, heavily infested moose are probably less vigilant and poorer at detecting approaching predators than are moose with few ticks. There are no data on this for winter ticks and moose, but Mooring and Hart (1995) documented that African impala, involved in grooming against ticks, responded several seconds later than non-grooming impala to a human who began walking slowly toward several impala when a grooming bout began. Four to eight seconds might not seem long to us, but give a wolf or cougar that much extra time as they stalk a moose, and

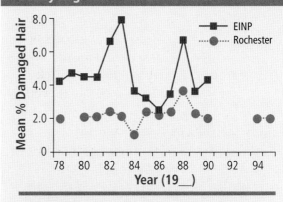

FIGURE 6.9. Yearly average tick-induced hair loss for a moose population at Elk Island National Park (EINP), near Edmonton, and a population near Rochester, Alberta, approximately 100 kilometres north of Edmonton. It is not known if the Rochester population actually has more ticks, but they groom more. [DATA FOR 1994-1995 FROM SKORUPKA 1999].

their chances of success likely improve a lot.

2. Compulsive licking, scratching and rubbing also rob moose of time normally spent feeding (see below).

3. It takes energy to lick and scratch. Details of this are not known and one might assume that this cost is small, but consider this: when moose groom, they groom in bouts. A bout is one sequence of licking, scratching, rubbing or shaking. For example, when a moose begins to lick, it does not lick once with its tongue, but rather goes through a number of licks. Each lick could be termed an episode and some to many episodes make up a bout of grooming. We determined that the hour spent grooming each day by moose in Elk Island Park in March and April included an average 22, 13 and 7 bouts, and 271, 242 and 114 episodes, respectively, for calves, bulls and cows. Of course, these activities are spread irregularly throughout the 24-hour day, but nonetheless, this is one more energetic burden moose carry in late winter-early spring.

In an African study, Dr. Ben Hart and colleagues at the University of California–Davis, have shown (1992) that antelope typically lick against ticks up to 2000 times every 12 hours.

4. Feeding ticks and excessive grooming cause open wounds in the skin, which can result in secondary bacterial infection.

5. Grooming leaves the insulating winter coat of hair damaged or lost, thus resulting in loss of heat. One could assume that extensive loss of hair results in moose being exposed to thermal stress and increased metabolic demands and, in severe cold, hypothermia (see below).

To demonstrate the positive and negative sides of the grooming coin, graduate student Patricia Skorupka (1999) observed an adult bull groom 22 minutes non-stop in March. This moose had no visible loss of hair at the beginning of the observation period, but 9% of the hair coat on the lateral body surface was damaged at the end of the grooming session. A total of 44 grams (about $1/10$ pound) of hair was recovered from the snow where the moose had groomed. That hair contained 391 winter ticks, or, extrapolating to an hour of grooming each day, just over 1000 ticks each day.

■ (3) Reduced stored visceral fat

McLaughlin and Addison (1986) found that captive tick-infested moose, with extensive loss of winter hair coat, had less stored visceral fat than other moose. This was attributed in part to the increased energy costs of keeping warm in the face of the loss of heat from the denuded skin, and to bad weather.

It is tempting to speculate that hypothermia is common in ghost moose in the wild during very low temperatures. While this would probably be true if there were many ghost moose in January and February—when temperatures as low as minus 40° Celsius occur—in fact we see few ghosts at this time. The fact is that ticky moose groom most, hence lose most hair to become ghosts, in March and April, toward the end of winter.

Graduate student Dwight Welch and co-workers found (1990) that experimentally infested ticky moose had few metabolic problems during a mild winter, when winter-spring temperatures ranged from a low of minus 28° Celsius in February to a high of plus 14° Celsius in late April. They reasoned that moose simply do not lose much hair to grooming before March, and usually do not experience prolonged periods of severe cold after March.

■ (4) Decreased time feeding by moose as grooming time increases

Do blood-feeding winter ticks disrupt the normal feeding patterns of moose? This is not an easy question to answer, but there is a negative correlation between rate of grooming and time spent feeding by moose in March and April; that is, as grooming time increases, feeding time decreases. This might be a simple correlation rather than cause and effect, but moose definitely become preoccupied with grooming in late winter and early spring. And, if feeding time is compromised to allow grooming, moose either consume less forage or spend less time trying to find the most nutritious food items.

Being preoccupied by biting ticks makes sense because March and April comprise the main time for feeding by ticks; that's when irritation and itch are at their peak. Thus, it can certainly be suggested that moose sacrifice feeding time in order to attempt to remove winter ticks. Either that or biting ticks cause moose to lose their appetite, as reported for other ticks on cattle.

Seldom are things of science black and white, and there is one more potentially complicating issue here. Most northern members of the deer family—deer, elk, caribou and moose— voluntarily reduce feeding in late winter. Such reductions are coincident with the fact that the quality of forage is relatively poor then. Nutritionists tell us

that this is associated with a seasonal decline in metabolic rate. It occurs yearly and has been reported for captive moose on high-quality diets. However, voluntarily decreased feeding seems to occur slightly earlier in winter than when ticks are causing most problems, and is followed by a rapid increase in food intake.

Whatever the reasons, moose experience the greatest problems from ticks, and eat relatively poor quality food, at the time of year when they can least afford it. Mooring and Samuel (1999) state: "It is possible that a poor nutritional plane during March and April makes moose more susceptible to the debilitating effects of heavy tick infestation, lowers the energy reserves available for high rates of grooming, and increases the cost of replacing heat energy lost through a damaged hair coat. Under such nutritional restrictions, tick infestation, grooming, and hair loss would result in higher costs than at other times of the year."

■ (5) Restlessness

The life of a moose in winter is normally one of eating, lying down (resting), and ruminating. Moose are well adapted to cold and one energetic advantage for moose on cold days is to remain bedded. In addition to grooming as an added activity, the itch associated with biting winter ticks appears to irritate moose to the point of affecting their normal daily activities, causing them to become restless. No conclusive data are available, but experimentally infested moose spent less time lying down than did moose with no ticks except during May and June, when moose have few if any ticks (FIGURE 6.10).

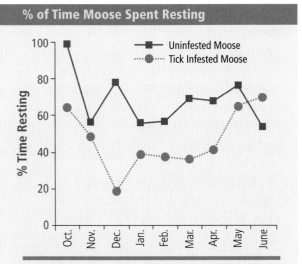

% of Time Moose Spent Resting

- ■— Uninfested Moose
- ○····· Tick Infested Moose

FIGURE 6.10. Moose with ticks are restless and spend less time lying down than moose with no ticks. Shown here is the percentage of observation time 13 captive moose infested with winter ticks, and 11 captive moose with no winter ticks, spent lying down. [MODIFIED FROM SAMUEL, 1991].

■ (6) Reduced growth of young moose

The logic here seems straightforward; tick-infested moose should eat less and, hence, their growth should be reduced. However, the few studies done show no clear pattern of results. Graduate student Vicky Glines (see Glines and Samuel, 1989) used two pairs of captive paired moose calves to examine their growth. Pairs were of the same sex and weight. Each pair included one animal infested with 31,000 tick larvae in autumn, and one not. Moose received a high quality, artificial diet. There was no difference in the mean daily food consumption between

infested and control moose, but one infested calf lost significantly more weight between March 12 and May 21 than its uninfested counterpart. The problem with this study, of course, was the small sample size.

McLaughlin and Addison (1986) stated that nine captive moose calves, experimentally infested with winter ticks and exhibiting extensive hair loss, "had much lower average weight-gains...than the other moose [those with little loss of hair]". In a 1993 paper dealing with the same calves, Addison and McLaughlin stated that they did not observe anorexia[16] in the calves that were given 20,000 to 42,000 tick larvae; in fact, the calves fed well. In 1994, Addison and colleagues presented data that suggested that winter ticks may have caused a reduction in body mass[17] of these young moose in autumn.

A combined assessment suggests that winter ticks do not depress appetite of captive moose, but one must use caution when extrapolating results to wild moose in that the captive moose in these studies were fed high-quality diets, and did not have to spend much time or energy acquiring food. Also, numbers of ticks on moose in both studies were generally low compared with numbers recorded for many wild moose.

In summary, winter ticks are invasive for moose; of that there is no doubt. Certain aspects of invasiveness proposed here need further study. How moose respond is next.

---

[16] Depressed appetite.

[17] Even though the terms "mass" and "weight" are often used interchangeably, if you are into fitness, you will know that weight deals with gravity, while mass is a relationship between body weight and other body composition measures. Fitness folks are interested in percent body fat as their measure of mass. Addison et al. (1994) looked at moose chest girth, total body length and shoulder height.

Moose grooming for ticks using tongue and teeth.

Behavioural strategies used by moose to evade winter ticks

■ Moose tac-*ticks*

A bit of a horse race has evolved between parasites and the hosts they attack. The parasite uses a variety of morphological, physiological and behavioural adaptations to improve its chances of finding, getting onto, or into, a host, and staying there to reproduce successfully. The behavioural adaptations ticks use to find and attach to moose are good examples of this.

Turnabout is fair play.

Hosts have evolved defences including immunological and behavioural responses that enable them to evade, thus, regulate the numbers of winter ticks. Such interactions often work well, or at least the relationship is stable, for both host and parasite. Equilibrium is established between parasite and host wherein numbers of parasites are relatively few on, or in, the host, and death of the host is rare. This occurs when host and parasite have been together a long time, and the giving and taking of advantage belongs to neither opponent. The horse race reaches a point where the result is a dead heat.

Grooming is probably the most important behavioural strategy used by moose against infestations of winter ticks, but moose are not nearly as efficient as bison, deer and elk at reducing tick numbers by grooming.

In other cases, it appears that the host has not yet evolved the necessary defence mechanisms to co-exist with the parasite without death to the host. Moose with winter ticks appear to fit this latter category. That is, moose use several strategies called "parasite avoidance strategies" to reduce the number of winter ticks, but these strategies are not very efficient, thus often leaving moose with too many ticks. Nonetheless, moose attempt to avoid or minimize exposure to winter ticks by:

1. avoiding clumps of tick larvae on vegetation in autumn;
2. tolerating magpies and other birds that sit on them and feed on ticks;
3. self-grooming to remove ticks.

■ Avoiding ticks

As moose and other wild ungulates move through and feed on vegetation, they are annually exposed to many thousands of winter tick larvae. And yet in some years we think they should be acquiring many more ticks than they do. As far-fetched as it might sound, we began to wonder if moose could detect and avoid those clumps of larvae on vegetation in autumn, thereby reducing exposure to tick larvae.

This is exactly what cattle in Australia do when exposed to larvae of a similar tick. Dr. Rob Sutherst and his colleagues reported (1986) that cattle either refused to graze in small experimental paddocks seeded with tick larvae, or they avoided small areas of pasture seeded with many tick larvae. In contrast, cattle in pastures with no ticks fed normally, showing no behavioural alterations. Photographs in the Sutherst paper show cattle changing direction abruptly on entering tick-infested circular plots in the pasture. Animals exhibited a state of increased alertness following apparent visual detection of the dark brown larvae on grass.

We set up a simpler experiment using a captive cow moose (Samuel and Welch, 1991). Two identical pails of alfalfa pellets were placed about one metre apart in an outdoor pen and several clumps of tick larvae were introduced on the pellets in one of the pails. The moose had been infested with winter ticks the year previous, so she had the experience of being bitten many times by feeding ticks. She was deprived of her usual food ration for 12 hours. Then she was offered the two pails of pelleted food, one of which was seeded with ticks.

In several identical trials, the cow moose eagerly approached the pails, moved her head to within 15 centimetres of each pail, and began feeding from the uninfested pail. She always became agitated when assessing the infested food and initially avoided the tick-infested food. When food had been consumed from the pail without ticks, she ate from the infested pail on rare occasion.

The sizes of the clumps of larvae on the alfalfa pellets were similar to sizes seen on vegetation in the wild, so the experiment was somewhat similar to what might happen in the wild. How moose detect larvae is not known, but we assume it is visually.

■ Magpies as tick busters

When two dissimilar organisms live together in close association, it is called symbiosis. If one of the two symbionts lives at the expense of the other, it is called parasitism. If both symbionts benefit, it is called mutualism.

The mutualistic relationship between oxpeckers—the world's only bird that feeds exclusively on ticks—and their African mammalian hosts is well known. Red-billed and yellow-billed oxpeckers gain a major food item by eating ticks from animals such as impala, eland, giraffe, sable, zebra and rhinos. These hosts benefit from improved health by allowing oxpeckers to feed on them. In a sense the system comprises a predator (the oxpecker) and a parasitic prey (the ticks). The system is efficient; oxpeckers commonly have 400 ticks in their stomach and they often remove over 90% of the ticks (see Mooring and Mundy, 1996).

One might predict that some species of African vertebrates, with large numbers of ticks, have evolved behaviour facilitating foraging by oxpeckers. Indeed, oxpeckers are known to forage on the largest available hosts that support higher densities of ticks than smaller hosts. They also feed primarily on parts of the body such as ears, neck and around the anus, that hosts such as impala cannot reach by oral grooming; that's where tick densities are highest.

Moose, elk, bighorn sheep and mule deer are like African ungulate hosts in that they tolerate birds to perch and feed on them. In Alberta, black-billed magpies and the occasional gray jay are seen on these animals. Birds usually perch on the back,

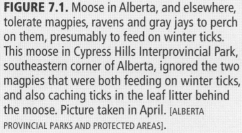

FIGURE 7.1. Moose in Alberta, and elsewhere, tolerate magpies, ravens and gray jays to perch on them, presumably to feed on winter ticks. This moose in Cypress Hills Interprovincial Park, southeastern corner of Alberta, ignored the two magpies that were both feeding on winter ticks, and also caching ticks in the leaf litter behind the moose. Picture taken in April. [ALBERTA PROVINCIAL PARKS AND PROTECTED AREAS].

FIGURE 7.2. Twin mule deer fawns in Waterton Lakes National Park being attended by two magpies apparently feeding on winter ticks. [FRANK DE BOON, WITH PERMISSION ALCES].

but they also cling to the sides and feed on ticks.

Each year in Alberta, magpies are presented with an abundant, but temporary, source of food in March and April: blood-feeding adult winter ticks. In eastern Canada, other members of the Corvidae family, such as common ravens and gray jays, take advantage of the same abundance of winter ticks (see Addison and others, 1989).

These birds both attend and feed on hosts such as moose, elk and mule deer, or forage on the ground near a feeding moose or at a moose-bedding site (FIGURES 7.1 and 7.2). It is common to see magpies land on moose, or at moose bedding sites, seemingly foraging (= pecking) in the hair and snow, respectively, for ticks. I have observed up to three magpies feeding on a moose. During one such observation, a magpie appeared to be removing ticks from the moose and caching them in footprints made by the moose in the snow.

This interaction is different from the better-known oxpecker-tick-African vertebrate system in that magpies do not depend entirely on ticks for food. Magpies are simply opportunistic feeders on ticks. During March and April, when ticks are abundant in the environment, magpies and jays likely switch behaviour and feed extensively on ticks. Those ticks not eaten are probably cached in leaf litter to be eaten later. This behaviour is called "scatter hoarding", which means that magpies prepare for future needs by storing excess food gathered in times of food abundance at scattered locations.

In an outdoor laboratory study (Samuel and Welch, 1991), captive magpies were offered a choice of dogfood or winter ticks. Dogfood is the preferred food of magpies in captivity and many dog owners would agree that magpies like dogfood. Results showed that magpies first ate, then cached, a lot of ticks and dogfood pellets. When caching ticks, the birds would collect a few ticks in their mouths, then fly to a ground site where they cached ticks in leaf and grass litter. Magpies tended to cache more ticks than they ate; one bird cached 24 ticks in 10 minutes.

But the startling finding was that magpies cached live ticks rather than killing them first. This means that if magpies do not return to feed on this food source, ticks might well survive to lay eggs and produce next year's crop of ticks.

Trost (1999) presented a good, brief review of magpies. Apparently, scatter-hoarding of food by magpies is usually only a short-term strategy; food items are recovered within a few days. Magpies have good short-term memory. The portion of the brain used for short-term memory, the hippocampus, is relatively large. Cache sites are remembered using sight or smell.

How does this relate to the health and well-being of moose? Obviously, in the short term, it is advantageous for moose to let magpies remove ticks from them, whether the ticks are eaten or cached. Same holds for magpies. They benefit from the highly nutritious diet of winter ticks. However, magpies might also benefit in the long term, if they do not soon use their caches (that is, before early June when ticks lay eggs for the next generation). If caches go uneaten, there is the potential for increased survival and dispersal of engorged female ticks, and larger tick populations to harass moose and feed magpies the next year.

Consider also that magpies cache ticks alive in ideal habitat (that is, in moist, protected areas in litter) for ticks to survive and produce offspring.

Unfortunately, the number of cached ticks recovered and eaten by magpies is unknown. However, the availability of natural food for magpies of central Alberta has been shown to be in short supply in March and April, the time of nest building and egg laying. Ticks, including those cached, may be an important locally abundant food source for magpies at this time.

Magpies have been shown to nest earlier, and in greater numbers, when a single rich amount of food is available early in breeding season. Winter ticks could be that rich pulse of food for magpies.

Perhaps complicating this picture is the fact that magpies are territorial and cache their food in their territories. A magpie would not be expected to venture far outside its territory, especially during the breeding season, to collect ticks from a moose. However, a magpie might be expected to collect and cache as many ticks as it can when a tick-infested moose moves through its territory.

While it is clear that winter ticks present an important, locally abundant food source for magpies in March and April, it is unclear if predation on ticks by magpies diminishes or enhances population growth of ticks. Nor is it clear whether or not tick predation has, as a consequence, an indirect positive, or negative, impact on moose populations. Future research should investigate this potentially important relationship. Studies are also needed to determine whether magpies are like oxpeckers and feed preferentially on the large-sized hosts (such as moose), with the highest densities of ticks, rather than smaller animals, in this case deer or elk with fewer ticks. Magpies might choose to minimize search time for ticks by feeding on the more social elk that often occur in groups, rather than moose that tend to be solitary.

Because of the presence of the hump, moose cannot groom certain areas of the body as can deer and elk. One might suggest that magpies take advantage of this by feeding preferentially on areas of the body where moose cannot groom and thus, where tick densities are highest.

Magpies would seem not to lose in this interaction. If they disseminate ticks through caching, and larger tick populations result, then ticks may present a more abundant food source in subsequent years. Alternatively, moose die-offs could occur resulting in moose carcasses for magpies to scavenge.

It is not known how long winter ticks, moose and magpies have co-existed. The association is probably recent. When bison were widespread and abundant, so too were magpies. Magpies frequently followed Native Americans as they pursued bison, living on refuse of those hunts. When bison numbers plummeted, magpie numbers dropped, too. Interactions of magpies and moose in Alberta probably occurred with the breakup of the boreal forest by settlement in recent times. Although the early history of winter ticks causing problems for moose is not known for Alberta, tick-related moose die-offs occurred in the early 1930s in Elk Island National Park, and elsewhere.

Magpies, being a species that relies heavily on agriculturally produced carrion, at least in Alberta, probably became numerous as the agricultural industry grew. As numbers of winter ticks became numerous on moose, magpies likely became more predatory on this extensive, transitory food source. In a sense, this is a relatively new story. If so, the ecological and evolutionary implications of this three-partner symbiosis may not yet be resolved.

■ Grooming by moose to remove ticks: being *tick*-ed off

Animals groom as part of their way of caring for their body surface. It has a variety of functions including communication, maintaining social relationships, maintaining insulation and removal of parasites. Moose basically have few ectoparasites besides ticks, so grooming is probably the main behavioural strategy used by moose against winter ticks.

Grooming was described in the previous chapter, because it is the reason the winter hair coat of moose is often partially-to-completely destroyed. All animals with ticks likely groom against ticks, but strategies of grooming appear to differ among species of animals.

One might assume that all animals under attack from ticks would try to maximize removal of ticks by grooming, while at the same time, expending as little energy as possible doing so. If winter ticks are as invasive for moose as I suggest, moose should have evolved strategies that efficiently remove ticks at little cost to moose. This implies eliminating or greatly reducing tick numbers before or just after they attach to moose in autumn; that is, before ticks extract a lot of blood from moose.

The question is: How successful is grooming by moose for ticks, especially when compared with other hosts such as elk and bison? As it turns out, success is relative. Recall the large numbers of ticks on moose compared with the smaller tick loads on elk, bison and deer. Also recall that moose groom most in March and April in response to the life stages of winter ticks, nymphs and adults, which take a lot of blood.

In the evolutionary arms race between ticks and hosts, hosts either groom preventatively so that few ticks establish, or they groom in response to tick bite. Preventative tick-grooming has been reported for a number of species including impala and other African antelope, bison and elk. In these species, the grooming response appears to operate like a clock, with periodic bouts of grooming that remove ticks prophylactically, *before* they can attach and feed on blood.

The mechanism for this type of host response has been termed "programmed grooming" by Dr. Ben Hart and colleagues (1992) at the University of California–Davis. Its use would appear to be more adaptive than grooming only *after* being bitten—or fed upon—by ticks. A key prediction of the programmed grooming model is that those animals that groom the most will have the fewest ticks, ticks having been removed by preventive grooming. Programmed groomers would be expected to remove winter ticks early on in the life of the infestation, that is—in the case of winter ticks—removing larvae in autumn.

Alternatively, if hosts do not groom preventatively, but rather in response to tick bite, the mechanism is termed "stimulus grooming". With this model, one would predict that a host with the most ticks, thus the most stimulation or itch sensation from tick bite, will groom the most. In other words, the grooming rate is directly proportional to the amount of irritant injected into the host from the salivary glands of the biting ticks. And, because moose concentrate most of their grooming in February, March and April, when ticks are consuming a relatively large amount of

blood, they are termed stimulus groomers.

It has been estimated that an adult female tick that has completed feeding on blood weighs over 100 times more than an adult female tick that has not fed on blood. Mooring and Samuel (1998a) proposed that, by extrapolation, the blood-fed adult female has 100 times more salivary secretions than does an unfed adult female. If one assumes a similar weight difference between each life stage of the tick—larva, nymph, adult—then each succeeding life stage might represent a minimum of 100 times more volume of saliva in their glands, that is, 100 times more stimulation to groom. Thus, the blood-fed adult female has 100 times more saliva secretions than that of the unfed adult female, which has 100 times that of the nymph, which has 100 times that of the larva. By default, the blood-feeding adult female tick might then be capable of injecting one million times more saliva than an engorging larva. I doubt these proportions hold in the real world, so this might be a far-fetched extrapolation, but you get the idea.

Of course, since grooming removes ticks, the result of both stimulus-driven and programmed grooming is fewer ticks on the animal. There is, though, a major difference between the two models. In the first instance, once the ticks have been groomed off the hide or, "full as a tick" they have dropped from the host, the itch-stimulus of the bite no longer exists and so stimulus-driven grooming ends; whereas, if the response is programmed, then programmed grooming should continue at the same rate, even when the biting stimulus has ceased. Simply put, hosts

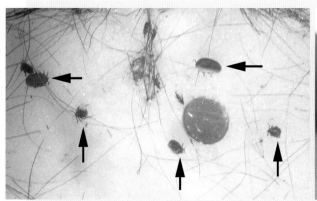

FIGURE 7.3. Grooming moose dislodge both hair and ticks (arrows) in March and April. (Nickel shown for scale). Moose often rub against vegetation leaving dislodged hair on vegetation.

that are programmed groomers regulate tick numbers at a manageable number; stimulus groomers do not. Or, are we on the wrong track here?

Moose that groom certainly remove ticks. Graduate student Patricia Skorupka (1999) observed moose in Elk Island National Park grooming in March and April, then collected dislodged hair and winter ticks from the snow at the grooming site (FIGURE 7.3). Seventeen moose groomed 1.95 hours in total during March and April and a total of 417 ticks was recovered at grooming sites. This extrapolates to a removal rate of between 3 and 4 ticks per minute of grooming and that seems like a lot of ticks.

Moose in Elk Island Park groomed an average of 1 hour per day in March and April, 1995 (Skorupka, 1999), which by extrapolation means that approximately 210 ticks could have been removed each day, and this translates into approximately 12,500 in the two months. Again, it seems like a lot of ticks. The question is: Does removing some 12,500 ticks in March and April, many of which are already consuming blood, mean much to a moose who might be hosting 50,000 ticks or more? Maybe yes, maybe no.

Before we follow this further, let's consider the grooming strategy of other Alberta hosts of winter ticks. Plains Bison and Wood Bison[18] (FIGURE 7.4) in Elk Island National Park share range with the more

FIGURE 7.4. Bison, both plains and wood bison, share range with moose in Elk Island National Park, but have few winter ticks.

[18] Plains Bison, *Bison bison bison*; Wood Bison, *Bison bison athabascae*.

heavily infested moose and elk, yet have few winter ticks (Mooring and Samuel, 1998b). Bison groomed significantly more in October than any month later in fall, winter, or early spring (FIGURE 7.5). Recall that October is when larval ticks are attaching to hosts from vegetation. In addition, newborn calves, in spring, groomed 15 to 20 times more frequently than adult females observed during the same period. Because the same tick density would be more costly to a smaller-

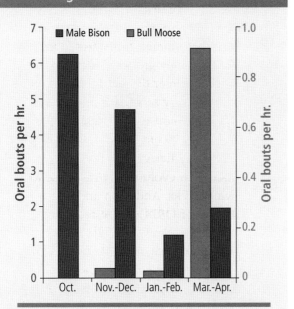

Grooming » Male Bison vs. Bull Moose

FIGURE 7.5. Bison tend to groom against winter ticks before or as they become infested by larvae in October and early November, and host few ticks over winter (see Mooring and Samuel, 1998b). In contrast, moose do little grooming until late in the infestation period, and host many ticks over winter.

bodied animal than a large one, smaller animals should groom more to maintain fewer ticks. These results support the concept of programmed grooming. At the least, stimulus grooming is not supported.

In addition, bison have extremely dense fur, with a thick, woolly undercoat. The resulting mat of hair, compared with that of deer, elk and moose, would present tick larvae with a barrier to movement to the skin surface.

How about elk? Mooring and Samuel (1998c) studied grooming behaviour of elk in Elk Island and Jasper national parks (FIGURE 7.6). Elk, like bison but not like moose, groomed most during October and November, when young ticks were attacking hosts from vegetation. Thus, like bison and impala, elk are programmed groomers, and mount an all-out grooming effort in the autumn to remove as many larval ticks as possible. Unlike moose, elk avoid the energy and thermoregulatory costs of intense grooming activity in the late winter and early spring.

Back to moose. In a 1974 review of parasites and diseases of moose, the late Dr. Roy Anderson, one of Canada's great parasitologists, and Dr. Murray Lankester, a former Professor at Lakehead University in Thunder Bay, Ontario, suggested that moose were poorly adapted to winter ticks. Specifically: "Moose may be much less successful than deer in removing the parasites [winter ticks] by rubbing and grooming behavior."

In 1991, Welch and co-workers infested small numbers of moose, elk, mule deer and white-tailed deer with larval winter ticks to determine the suitability of each of these hosts for winter ticks. Each host was infested with equivalent densities of ticks, one larva per square centimetre body surface. Immediately after infestation, white-tailed deer licked the small sites on their back where larvae had been placed. Within 48 hours these sites had no hair.

FIGURE 7.6. Elk grooming for ticks using tongue and teeth.

deer (0.6%) or white-tailed deer (0%). This points to efficient grooming by deer and elk, less efficiency by moose. Further indications of this were that female ticks that fed on moose were larger than ticks from other hosts, and hair damage and loss of hair was extensive only on moose.

In summary, grooming is probably the most important behavioural strategy used by moose against infestations of winter ticks, but moose are not nearly as efficient as bison, deer and elk at reducing numbers of ticks by grooming.

Why are moose an exception to the programmed-grooming model? Perhaps they groom ineffectively against winter ticks because, in an evolutionary sense, the association between moose and winter ticks is relatively recent. That is, there has been insufficient time for moose to mount an evolutionary response to winter ticks. Anderson and Lankester (1974) suggested that moose, a relatively recent arrival to North America, acquired winter ticks and other noxious parasites, from deer, the original host. This subject is explored in the next chapter.

In the spring, a higher percentage of engorged female ticks was recovered from moose (8.0%) than from elk (0.23%), mule

In summary, grooming is probably the most important behavioural strategy used by moose against infestations of winter ticks, but moose are not nearly as efficient as bison, deer and elk at reducing numbers of ticks by grooming.

White-tailed deer suffer little from winter tick infestation.

Speculating on the moose-winter tick arms race

■ Titan-*tick* struggle

If one examines the scientific literature and provincial and state government reports on the health of moose for the last 50 years or so, it becomes obvious that three parasites are particularly harmful to moose. They are:

1. winter tick, *Dermacentor albipictus*;
2. meningeal worm, *Parelaphostrongylus tenuis*;
3. large American liver fluke, *Fascioloides magna*.

Meningeal worm is also called brainworm, though the parasite does not normally live in the brain, but rather on the connective tissue coverings of the brain, the meninges. It is a roundworm that causes a neurologic disease known scientifically as parelaphostrongylosis, though the more popular name is moose sickness. The liver fluke causes disease of the liver known as fascioloidiasis or, more commonly, liver rot.

All three parasites are found in white-tailed deer, and, more importantly, all three are relatively harmless for whitetails, but pathogenic for moose.

We have dealt with winter ticks; let's look at the other two.

> White-tailed deer suffer little from parasites that cause problems for moose. Possible reasons for this are discussed here.

■ Meningeal Worm

Brain drain

Meningeal worm is one of the most studied parasites of North American wildlife because it causes such a severe neurologic disease in a variety of animals. It is a parasitic roundworm that occurs in most populations of white-tailed deer in eastern North America.

In Canada, meningeal worm has been reported from deer of Nova Scotia, New Brunswick, Quebec, Ontario, Manitoba and just into eastern Saskatchewan. Extending a line south from the Manitoba–Saskatchewan boundary provides an accurate western boundary for the United States.

Meningeal worm is transmitted from deer to deer, or deer to moose or other mammals, by way of land snails and slugs, which serve as intermediate hosts. Large mammals accidentally ingest infected snails and slugs during feeding.

When a deer eats an infected snail or slug, young meningeal worms leave the snail, penetrate the deer's stomach wall, enter the abdominal cavity and migrate to the spinal cord. Worms grow in the cord and move toward the brain,

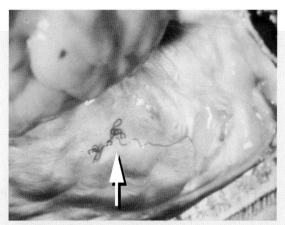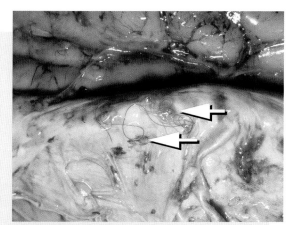

FIGURE 8.1. Meningeal worms live in the cranial cavity of many large, hoofed mammals of North America. They produce no ill effects or significant lesions in the normal host, white-tailed deer (left), but produce significant trauma (see dark hemorrhaging on brain and meninges of elk, right), and neurologic disease in many animals including moose. Meningeal worms are associated with the connective tissue coverings of the brain, the meninges. In both pictures, the meninges have been peeled back from the brain surface, which is at the top of both pictures, to expose the worms (arrows). [LEFT, ROY ANDERSON LAB; RIGHT, MARGO PYBUS, BOTH WITH PERMISSION OF STACKPOLE BOOKS].

eventually coming to rest on the meninges of the brain (FIGURE 8.1).

Migration in the spinal cord of white-tailed deer results in minor pathology. Seldom are white-tailed deer made ill by this parasite. Migration in the spinal cord and brain of moose and other large mammals can result in major tissue damage (FIGURE 8.1), neurologic disease and death.

Where infected white-tailed deer occur, so too can infection in other animals. This is because, on occasion, animals besides deer ingest infected snails.

Animals known to succumb to neurologic disease caused by meningeal worm include all North American members of the deer family: moose, elk, woodland caribou, black-tailed deer and mule deer, along with pronghorn antelope, introduced fallow deer, domestic goats, domestic sheep and llamas, plus a variety of captive exotic animals.

Moose sickness is an important disease, though its effect on eastern moose populations has been much debated in the literature. But there is no debate about whether or not meningeal worm is the cause of death in many individual moose. And it usually takes only a few worms to kill a moose. Moose sickness has been reported from Nova Scotia, New Brunswick, Quebec, Ontario, Manitoba, Saskatchewan, Maine, Minnesota and Michigan. Affected moose display a variety of signs including: weakness in the hindquarters, standing with weight forward on the front legs, ataxia (failure of muscular coordination), paresis (slight or incomplete paralysis), difficulty in rising, inability to stand, tilting or turning of the head and neck to one side, and circling (see Lankester, 2001 for more). Not a nice parasite. Not a nice disease.

Elk are more susceptible than white-tailed deer to acquiring neurologic

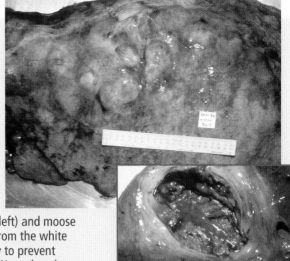

FIGURE 8.2. Liver fluke infection in white-tailed deer (left) and moose (right). The two adult flukes on the left were removed from the white fibrous capsule, which is produced by the host probably to prevent flukes from migrating and causing damage to the liver. Note that the surrounding liver tissue of this deer looks fine. Contrast that with the liver of the moose, which is markedly enlarged with extensive damage and fibrous tissue, and many young flukes (inset) that tend to migrate through, and destroy, liver tissue. [RIGHT AND INSET, MARGO PYBUS].

disease from infection with meningeal worm (see Samuel and colleagues, 1992), but appear to be less susceptible than moose.

There is no meningeal worm in Alberta, British Columbia, or Canada's northern territories. At one time it was suggested that meningeal worm would spread west naturally, but this has not happened. The most likely reason is that some ecological factor or factors, such as dry climate of the prairies of Alberta and Saskatchewan, limit the abundance of the snail hosts. Relatively low densities of deer in the west may also be involved (see Wasel and co-authors, 2003 for more).

■ Liver Fluke

Liver flukes are parasites known as trematodes, or flatworms. The one in moose, elk and deer is called the large American liver fluke. It is called "large" because it is LARGE, with adult flukes up to 8 centimetres long. It is easily

detected because of its size and the conspicuous damage inflicted on the liver of some of the animals it infects. Like meningeal worm and winter tick, liver fluke causes few problems for white-tailed deer, but some problems for moose (FIGURE 8.2).

Liver flukes are common in members of the deer and cattle families. Infected members in North America include deer, elk, caribou, cattle, domestic sheep and goat, and of course, moose.

Liver fluke infection is associated with water because it is transmitted from mammal to mammal via water snails. Thus, infection does not occur in the relatively dry Great Plains of North America, but rather along much of coastal southeastern United States, the northwest including Vancouver Island and coastal Washington and Oregon, around the Great Lakes, northern Quebec and Labrador and, perhaps strangely, on both sides of the continental divide in southern Alberta and British Columbia. In Alberta the main focus is in the mountains and foothills from Jasper National Park to the Montana border, with small pockets in Alberta in Cypress Hills Interprovincial Park and Elk Island National Park, and in central Saskatchewan.

An interesting sidelight to the distribution of this fluke in North America and Europe is how it appears in new places from time to time. For example, liver flukes appeared in Elk Island National Park about 15 years ago, and it now infects a high percentage of the elk population, and some moose. This is an important find because elk from this Park are a source for many reintroduction programs in the prairie provinces, and eastern Canada and the United States.

How it got there is anyone's guess. Perhaps it arrived with a wandering waterfowl from the Alberta hotspot, Banff National Park area, with an infected water snail accidentally lodged in its feathers. Lakes and the many sloughs in Elk Island have appropriate aquatic snails that serve as intermediate hosts. Perhaps a fluke-infected white-tailed deer made a long-distance trek to the Park, though Dr. Margo Pybus, a wildlife disease specialist with the Alberta Fish and Wildlife Division in Edmonton, states in a 2001 review, that "white-tailed deer do not appear to spread *F. magna*". Whatever the source, this parasite is now doing very well in Elk Island National Park.

Liver flukes were once common in another federal park, now known as Camp Wainwright, near the town of Wainwright in east-central Alberta. The present Camp was once Buffalo National Park, founded in the early 1900s. It was a refuge for large numbers of plains bison brought there primarily from Montana. Shortly thereafter, a small number of elk were brought to the Park from Banff and Montana. Whether or not native deer in the Wainwright area had liver flukes or, at some point, liver fluke was introduced to the area, is not known. The Park was fenced and, by 1920, held 7000 bison, numerous elk, yak (to cross with bison), and some local moose and mule deer. Soon thereafter, liver flukes were detected in bison.

Then, just before the Second World War, when the Park was being transformed into the Army Camp it is today, 2918 bison, 1806 elk, 113 moose and 242 deer were killed because of high infections with tuberculosis and liver flukes (see Lothian, 1981). Apparently, owing to the major effort to eliminate liver fluke, involving the use of copper sulfate to kill the aquatic snail intermediate hosts, and massive reductions of vertebrate hosts, liver flukes disappeared. Many of the lakes in the Park/Camp, that once held infected water snails, are still there today; the snails are *still* there; the deer, elk and moose are *still* there; but the parasite is gone. (Admittedly, elk and moose pretty well disappeared for some years, but are now back and doing well there.)

One of the earliest documented translocations of a pathogenic parasite (Bassi, 1875) exemplifies the relative ease with which liver flukes can become established in new areas where hosts, usually elk, are transplanted. In the 1860s the King of Italy introduced elk from North America to one of his game parks near Turin. The park had native red deer, perhaps fallow deer, introduced Indian Sambar deer and the

Indian Nilgai, or bluebull (a large antelope). It also had domestic sheep and goats. In 1872, the King's veterinarian, Dr. R. Bassi, began finding dead animals of several species of wild "deer" and domestic sheep and goats with major liver complications and a "new liver parasite". He described the parasite as *Distoma magnum*, now known as the large American liver fluke with the scientific name *Fascioloides magna*. Today this liver fluke continues to be a problem for native wildlife in Italy and other parts of Europe.

The life cycle of liver fluke involves large mammals and aquatic snails. Adult flukes mate in the liver of the infected vertebrate host and eggs move down the bile ducts to the intestine and are shed with the feces. If this occurs in water, eggs hatch to a swimming life-stage known as miracidia, which penetrate the foot of aquatic snails where they develop and multiply. One miracidium will become 1000 infective stages (cercaria) that leave the snail, swim to the surface and attach to vegetation at the air-water interface. They become like a cyst on the vegetation and there they wait for an elk, moose, deer, cow or sheep to eat them with the vegetation. Once eaten and swallowed they penetrate the wall of the intestine and move to and penetrate the liver. Like meningeal worm, adults live and produce young for years.

Reasons why liver flukes are benign in white-tailed deer, but not-so-benign in moose, relate to the extent of liver damage caused by immature migrating flukes in each host. Whitetails are a

> The King of Italy introduced liver flukes to Europe when he imported infected elk from North America in the 1860s. Today this liver fluke continues to be a problem for native wildlife in Italy and other parts of Europe.

normal host in which the parasite matures quickly, keeping worm migration and resulting liver damage to a minimum. Bile ducts remain unblocked, so that eggs produced by adult flukes can escape the liver and later exit the host via the feces.

Dr. Pybus (2001) categorized the moose as a "dead-end host". Immature flukes reach the liver of dead-end hosts, but seldom mature to breed. Rather, they continue to wander through the liver. Livers of dead-end hosts are infiltrated with fibrous tissue that develops in place of damaged tissue in the liver. This is the host's way of trying to stop flukes from migrating. Even if flukes mature and breed, eggs are blocked from leaving the liver because of extensive fibrous damage.

Liver flukes were first mentioned as a problem in moose (from northern Minnesota) in the early 1930s. Pat Karns (1972) estimated that almost 90% of livers of healthy-looking, hunter-killed moose in northwestern Minnesota were infected with flukes, and one-third of liver tissue was necrotic. In the same region, 50% of liver tissue was necrotic in moose that died of natural causes.

Disease in moose occurs only in those areas where moose share range with infected white-tailed deer or elk. Elk, like deer, are considered to be a normal host, but if animals are heavily infected, liver damage can be extensive and some animals will die. This has happened in recent years near the town of Banff, Alberta.

■ Time *ticks* away

What might account for different host responses to these three parasites? Why are white-tailed deer seemingly well adapted to these parasites, yet moose are seemingly poorly adapted, hence, ravaged by them, with elk somewhere in between? There are no clear answers, but none of the parasites in question is native to Europe or Asia, indicating that moose acquired them in North America, likely from the native North American deer of the genus *Odocoileus*.

Acquisition by moose might have occurred thousands of years ago, by what I call "the evolutionary proposal", or it might have occurred within the last approximately 150 years by "the landscape ecology proposal". Either way it involves infected deer sharing their environment with moose (and elk), and passing parasites to them. The question is: When might this have occurred?

In an evolutionary sense there is much conjecture in the literature about when ancestors of modern moose and elk invaded North America from Siberia. Relative to deer, both are recent immigrants that likely crossed the land bridge (now submerged beneath the Bering Sea) that connected Asia to present-day Alaska during the late Wisconsin glacial period some 24,000 to 10,000 years ago,[19,20] then spread south as recently as the early Holocene,[21] approximately 10,000 years ago. Burns (1986; and personal communication, 2004) documented a 9900-year-old elk skeleton from a site along the Smoky River, near Peace River, Alberta. This is the oldest record for Alberta. Ancestors of white-tailed and mule deer, that is, members of the genus *Odocoileus*, first appeared in the fossil record in southern North America several million years ago.

The evolutionary proposal suggests that winter ticks, meningeal worm, liver flukes and deer (genus *Odocoileus*) have become co-adapted due to a long evolutionary relationship. Then, in more recent thousands of years, they moved into moose habitat with their parasites, and moose became infected (TABLE 8.1). As Dr. Murray Lankester stated in a 1987

TABLE 8.1 Comparative summary of winter ticks, meningeal worm and liver flukes in several hosts.

Animal host	Relative years in North America	Life cycle completed? winter ticks	Life cycle completed? meningeal worm	Life cycle completed? liver fluke	Relative pathogenicity winter ticks	Relative pathogenicity meningeal worm	Relative pathogenicity liver fluke
White-tailed deer	several million	Yes	Yes	Yes	None	None	Little
Elk	11,000-70,000	Yes	Rarely	Yes	Little to Moderate	Moderate	Moderate to Severe
Moose	10,000-24,000	Yes	No	No	Severe	Severe	Severe

---

[19] For more on this, see the following books or papers in the Bibliography: Bubenik (1997), Harington (2003), Mooring and Samuel (1998a), O'Gara and Dundas (2002) and Peterson (1955).

[20] Papers in Harington's annotated bibliography (2003) document the oldest North American radiocarbon-dated moose skeleton at 11,500 years (northern Yukon Territory) and the oldest elk at 11,000 years (Alaska).

[21] The last 11,000 years of earth's history and the time since the last ice age.

FIGURE 8.3. Clearing land for agriculture is an ongoing activity at the southern edges of the boreal mixedwood forests of Alberta, Saskatchewan, and elsewhere in Canada. This activity attracts white-tailed deer, placing them in sympatry with moose.

review of parasites and diseases of moose: "White-tailed deer have probably extended their range northwards into moose habitat on numerous occasions during the past 10,000 years."[22]

The troublesome part of the "evolutionary proposal" is that one would expect moose, by now, to be more resistant to the ravages of these parasites given the many generations of co-adaptation that would have occurred between moose and parasite over the several thousand years of the "arms race" between them.

The "landscape ecology proposal" suggests that the relationship between moose and these three parasites is much more recent, perhaps something in the order of approximately 125 to 150 years. The area of most significant overlap of white-tailed deer and moose would have begun to occur as a result of extensive deforestation and land-clearing by humans in the last half of the 1800s in eastern North America; this at the southern limits of the Boreal Forest (for example, around the Great Lakes and St. Lawrence River). Deer would have been attracted to the region of early successional vegetation, the aftermath of logging and land clearing for agriculture, just as they are attracted today to farm-forest edges in the landscape (FIGURE 8.3). With the overlap, parasite exchange could have occurred.

---

[22] Dr. Lankester attributes this idea to his mentor, Dr. Roy C. Anderson.

This idea makes some sense in that the earliest records of moose suffering from these parasites occurred in eastern North America between the late 1860s and 1920. Obviously, winter ticks were on moose by the mid-19th century, because they were described from moose of Nova Scotia in 1869. Meningeal worm was not described from white-tailed deer until 1945, but records of moose sickness began appearing in the early 20th century, in northern Minnesota, along with reports of winter ticks and liver flukes on and in moose, respectively.

Meningeal worms, as well as liver flukes, cannot perpetuate themselves in moose, or at least are poor at doing so. Few meningeal worms mature in moose and few, if any, larvae are shed in moose feces. Most liver flukes do not mature in moose, so no eggs are shed in moose feces. Thus, in practical terms, moose are dead-end hosts. For moose to acquire meningeal worm or liver fluke, they must share range with infected white-tailed deer (for meningeal worm) and whitetails, mule deer, black-tailed deer, caribou, or elk (for liver flukes).

No matter which proposal one accepts, if either, the give-and-take of the arms race apparently has not persisted long enough for moose to mount an effective defence. Each parasite appears to hold to a principle proposed by Dr. John Holmes (1982), former professor at the University of Alberta, that parasites often spread from a host in which it has a relatively long association (that is, a host that is well adapted to the parasite and in which the parasite is relatively benign), to a new host with which it has had a relatively short association (that is, a host that is poorly adapted and in which the parasite is relatively pathogenic).

What might the future bring? It is possible that there will be no long-term change for moose with meningeal worm and liver fluke; that

Perhaps winter ticks spread from

| White-tailed deer
that have these characteristics | TO | Moose
with these characteristics |
|---|---|---|
| **Long** association with winter ticks | | **Short** association with winter ticks |
| **Well** adapted | | **Poorly** adapted |
| **Benign** | | **Pathogenic** |
| **Few ticks** per deer | | **Many ticks** per moose |
| **Few** deer die | | **Many** moose die |
| **Selective advantage for reduced pathogenicity** | | **No selective advantage for reduced pathogenicity** |

is, there might be no selection for reduced pathogenicity (see Holmes 1996). The reason is that, with the exception of elk and their liver flukes, these parasites depend only on white-tailed deer for transmission and survival. They do not complete their life cycle in moose; so there is no evolutionary reason for the parasite to become less pathogenic in them.

This is not so for winter ticks. Winter ticks complete their life cycle on moose, elk, deer, caribou, etc. This might be why we see some adaptive mechanisms at work in moose to avoid or reduce numbers of winter ticks.

In summary, in the real world, parasites like winter ticks, meningeal worms and liver flukes, have evolved ways to invade hosts like moose, elk and deer. Hosts, in turn, have evolved defences, often behavioural or immunological, to regulate numbers of invading parasites. At best, both parasite and host do pretty well. At worst, when the defences are not efficient, many hosts die.

Grooming is probably the most important behavioural strategy used by moose against infestations of winter ticks, but moose are not nearly as efficient as deer or elk at reducing numbers of ticks by grooming. It appears that winter ticks might have spread from deer, the more widespread and numerous host, to moose, in which there is little selection for reduced pathogenicity. Much of what is presented here is speculative, but it seems to make biological sense.

Winter ticks might have spread from deer, the more widespread and numerous host, to moose, in which there is little selection for reduced pathogenicity.

In spite of winter ticks, moose populations are doing well throughout Alberta and Canada.

Managing winter ticks,
a s-*tick*-y problem

Moose are host to an unusually large number of winter ticks. Die-offs of moose, associated with, or attributed to, winter ticks, are widespread and have occurred since the early part of the last century. Several questions arise. Can winter ticks alone kill moose? Can something be done to manage or control tick numbers?

The first question is difficult to answer because moose do not live in a bubble, but rather in a variable, changing environment with a variety of stresses that can interact to cause death. But, I know of no moose die-offs where winter ticks were felt to be the only contributing factor. Main contributing factor? Often. Only contributing factor? Probably never.

A combination of factors is involved in most, probably all, tick-associated die-offs of moose, with winter severity, moose densities and food quality and quantity being mentioned most often. For example, severe winters cause nutritional problems for moose that could weaken the immune response and cause them to be more susceptible to effects of winter ticks. If, though, all known mortality factors were absent, and a moose population were generally free of stress, I would guess that

> Moose habitat and numbers, along with weather, appear to be important determinants of tick numbers.

80,000 to 100,000 ticks would be lethal for moose, particularly calves, no matter how good the food supply or how mild the winter.

Ticks are managed at an appropriate low level in many domestic animal situations, suggesting that approaches used to control ticks in domestic animals could be applied to moose populations. A herd of cattle in a certain paddock, having problems with ticks, can be treated with insecticides (called acaricides), or moved to another paddock (called pasture spelling). Either of these manipulations could break the tick's life cycle of transmission. These are hardly techniques applicable to moose, which are not exactly herding animals.

Insecticides are often applied to livestock as a skin drench, or by injection, to purge them of ticks. Ear tags impregnated with acaricide, or sustained-release, drug-filled boluses, inserted into the rumen of livestock that can release a steady rate of drug daily for many weeks, also work well. These techniques would not work for moose populations in the wild, though I get suggestions every year from someone who has magically devised a way to get chemical treatments to

FIGURE 9.1.
Natural and prescribed fires in spring kill winter ticks.
[PARKS CANADA, ELK ISLAND NATIONAL PARK].

moose.[23] Even if there were ways to get acaricides to moose, the manipulation would have to be done every year, because moose lose and reacquire ticks yearly. In the end, a little common sense is good for the soul.

Trying to manage or control ticks on wild moose is complicated, because it entails trying to determine the component factors that account for high numbers of ticks and resulting moose die-offs, then seeing if there are ways to intervene to reduce numbers of ticks. We already know there are some natural controls in place that reduce tick numbers:

- moose detect larvae on vegetation and avoid them;
- moose self-groom to remove ticks;
- magpies eat and cache ticks.

All three reduce numbers of ticks to some degree on moose, but if these are pieces to the puzzle, they seem to be relatively small ones, because none has had significant long-term effects on the overall size of tick populations in the environment. Or, to put it another way, numbers of ticks on moose remain high, at least at periodic intervals.

Other, perhaps more important, factors involved in determining numbers of ticks are discussed next.

■ Burn those rascals

How about fire?

Fire, often in the form of prescribed burning, has been shown to kill ticks (FIGURE 9.1). Such fire must occur at the right time of year in order to kill ticks; that is, when ticks are off host animals. The two best times of year to kill winter ticks by fire are in late winter–early spring, when adult female winter ticks have dropped from moose to lay their eggs, and in autumn, when tick larvae are on vegetation.

---

[23] One person, who wanted to take advantage of the fact that moose like to use natural salt licks in spring, pushed strongly to "put drugs in salt blocks and, each spring, scatter those blocks throughout moose habitat of Alberta from the air". Cost was obviously not a consideration.

The type of fire is also important; slow, hot fires work best. Female winter ticks seek the duff layer when they drop from moose. Duff is the spongy layer of decomposing vegetation beneath the leaf litter on the forest floor. Burning often removes the leaf litter, but not the duff layer. It takes a slow, hot fire to burn the duff layer and, hence, to kill female ticks in spring.

Elk Island National Park has had a prescribed spring burning program for some 25 years. In addition, a natural fire burned over 12% of the Park in May 2004. Spring fires, natural or prescribed, kill many female ticks on the ground before they lay eggs. Results of a study by Drew and others (1985) in Elk Island Park, revealed that an estimated 97% of female ticks, released in eight habitat types on May 3, died during a slow, hot, prescribed burn on May 12. In contrast, 60% of females survived at sites not burned.

One can only guess at the overall effect this has on tick populations. If, for example, the 12% of Elk Island that burned in spring 2004 happened to be preferred habitat for moose, there might be significant reductions of ticks to attack moose in autumn 2004.

Fire across North American moose habitat might have had long-term effects on ticks in decades past, and before fire suppression. In Alberta, fires were extensive and common, a natural part of the landscape history. Even with fire suppression, recent weather has brought dry conditions, and widespread spring and summer fire, to Alberta and the west. Such fires kill many ticks and the eggs they lay. But the aftermath of fire often leads to more moose.

Fire in the boreal forest creates what has been described as "transient habitat" for moose, because moose are attracted to abundant shrub vegetation created by fire

(summarized by Telfer, 1984). Winter tick production is higher in shrub vegetation communities (that is, those habitats created by logging or fire) than in spruce forest (see Chapter 4).

In summary, fire likely has immediate, negative effects on winter tick populations, and rather immediate, positive effects on moose populations; but critical research is needed to put detail to this subject. Gut feelings suggest that the effects of fire are local and probably short-term insofar as having a major impact on tick numbers.

■ Habitat

There appears to be a habitat component to survival and development of winter ticks when they are in the leaf litter in late spring and summer. Aspen-dominated forests appear to be good habitats for winter ticks and moose, while winter ticks do poorly in spruce forests (discussed in Chapter 4). This might partially explain why winter ticks are a scourge for moose in the aspen-rich Peace River country of northwestern Alberta and nearby British Columbia, and also along the southern fringe of the boreal forest of Alberta.

However, the overall evidence suggests that numbers of moose, or moose densities, and weather are the two main drivers of tick numbers.

■ Manage ticks by managing numbers of moose

It is intuitive that numbers of ticks should vary according to numbers of moose. As moose numbers increase in a local area, tick numbers should follow. The general pattern is that more tick bites lead to more itching and more grooming by moose, which leads to more hair damage and loss, with possibly concurrent suppression of appetite and feeding by moose. Lower appetite and reduced foraging by moose could lower the energy reserves available for high rates of grooming, and increase the cost of replacing heat energy lost through a damaged hair coat.

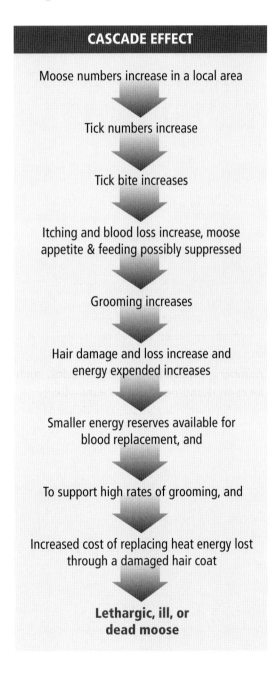

CASCADE EFFECT

Moose numbers increase in a local area

Tick numbers increase

Tick bite increases

Itching and blood loss increase, moose appetite & feeding possibly suppressed

Grooming increases

Hair damage and loss increase and energy expended increases

Smaller energy reserves available for blood replacement, and

To support high rates of grooming, and

Increased cost of replacing heat energy lost through a damaged hair coat

Lethargic, ill, or dead moose

Long-term data that track numbers of ticks and numbers of moose are both difficult and expensive to collect, but have been collected in Elk Island National Park, where officials keep close track of moose numbers, and we tracked numbers of ticks for some years (FIGURE 9.2).

In the 1980s, average numbers of ticks on moose kept pace with moose numbers, though there was a one-year lag. As moose numbers increased, so too did tick numbers, and vice versa. There were two periods of moose die-offs in the early and late 1980s. Many moose died when numbers of moose peaked at nearly 400, or about 2.9 moose per square kilometre, in the main part of the Park, and average numbers of ticks peaked at 50,000 to 60,000 ticks. This suggests that moose density—as expressed by the availability of vegetation, that is, food for moose—and numbers of ticks are important in determining moose abundance at Elk Island National Park.

When moose are few in number, following a die-off, they are soon in good physical condition and in good health due to abundant vegetation on which to feed. They have relatively few ticks. Moose numbers can increase rapidly, especially in Elk Island Park, where there are no wolves or bears. More moose provide more habitat on which ticks can develop, so tick numbers increase. In several years, moose increase to a point where they saturate the environment with ticks that can be picked up the next year. Then, the high-density moose population begins to experience a decline in body condition and health, because of deteriorating food supply and high numbers of ticks. Moose begin to die. Significant losses usually occur over at least two winters because many ticks that occur on moose in year one, will drop off both living and dying moose and lay eggs that will become a good crop of young ticks over summer, then attack moose before the second winter.

Chuck Blyth, former Senior Park Warden at Elk Island Park, said it best in his 1995 thesis: "It appears that at Elk Island, ticks have reached high densities on moose

CORRELATION BETWEEN MOOSE NUMBERS AND TICK NUMBERS

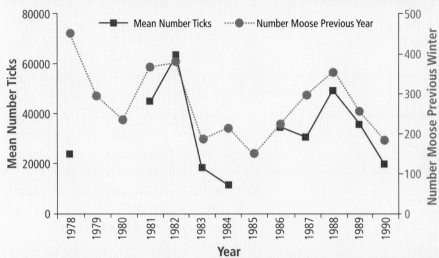

FIGURE 9.2. In general, tick numbers track moose numbers in Elk Island National Park. In this timeframe, when moose numbers approach 400 (approximately 2.9 moose per square kilometre) in the Main Park area, and ticks numbers approach 50,000 to 60,000 per moose, moose die.

following all major periods of moose increase…If the winter tick can influence moose condition and contribute to mortality [which they can] then ticks should be considered an important determinant of the form of [moose] density-dependence at Elk Island." Further, as explained earlier, moose are nutritionally stressed in winter, and winter ticks can further mediate this. Gladney and co-workers (1973) have shown that cattle on a lower plane of nutrition host more ticks. Further, moose may well be preoccupied with grooming when they should be eating.

In summary, controlling numbers of moose by hunting might be the best way to manage tick populations, or at least to moderate the effects of ticks on moose (FIGURE 9.3).

■ Weather as a factor influencing tick and moose numbers

If it is intuitive that numbers of moose influence numbers of ticks in the environment, then it is also intuitive that weather must play a role in influencing tick numbers, especially at high latitudes, such as central and northern Alberta—likely elsewhere across Canada—with cold

FIGURE 9.3. Hunting might be the best way to manage numbers of ticks on moose.

winters and cool springs. Weather should influence tick survival when ticks are off moose from late winter and spring, through summer and early-to-mid autumn. Does it?

Scientific research often involves good luck along the way, but most important findings are simply the result of good experimental design and hard work. Such a combination enabled graduate student Mark Drew (see Drew and Samuel, 1986) to discover that adult female winter ticks often died before laying eggs, when they dropped from moose onto snow in late winter and early spring. This suggests that long winters, with snow on the ground well into April, might kill enough ticks to reduce tick numbers on moose the following winter (FIGURE 9.4). In contrast, it also suggests that short, mild winters, with early snow melt, result in more female ticks producing young ticks to infest moose the next autumn.

So we know, or would predict, that:

- cold weather in late winter and spring should result in decreased survival of female ticks dropping from moose,

FIGURE 9.4. Long cold winters, with much snow, are hard on both moose and winter ticks. Many of the winter tick females that drop from moose onto snow in cold weather die.

while warm weather at this time should result in increased survival;
- cold weather in spring should result in decreased numbers of eggs laid; warm spring, the opposite;
- cold weather in summer should result in decreased numbers of eggs that hatch to larvae, while warm sunny weather, with some moisture to provide the high humidity in the duff layer that ticks need in summer, should result in the opposite;
- cold or snowy weather in autumn should reduce the activity and availability of larvae, while warm weather should extend the window of moose exposure to tick attack.

Evidence supporting these predictions is observational, not experimental, but the idea is gaining momentum (see Wilton and Garner, 1993). There were widespread die-offs of moose across North America from 1988 to 1990, and again in 1992 (reviewed in Chapter 2), attributed to winter ticks, the increasing numbers of which were thought to be driven by warm weather in the preceding late winters and early springs. Timmermann and Whitlaw (1992) suggested that ticks were responsible for synchronous population declines of moose in north-central Ontario, northeastern Minnesota and on Isle Royale, which were "triggered by short-term changes in weather patterns in the late 1980s".

Weather was thought to be the main factor that mediated the major tick-influenced 1999 die-offs of moose across Alberta and British Columbia, especially northern regions (reviewed in Chapter 2). There was reduced snow in Alberta during the winter-spring period preceding the die-off winter of 1998-1999, and summer was hot and autumn warm. Moose entered the winter of 1998-1999, stressed by less and relatively poor-quality food, deep snow and lots of ticks.[24]

---

[24] See Pybus (1999) for more on this die-off.

A few unrelated points on weather and ticks follow. We found an interesting twist when examining year-to-year changes in hair damage/hair loss in two moose populations in central Alberta that were about 150 km apart (data in Figure 6.9); annual hair loss was somewhat parallel between the two areas from 1978 to 1990. This suggests that, although numbers of ticks on moose can differ between moose populations, perhaps owing to differences in nutrition or densities of moose, year-to-year changes in tick populations can be similar. And this suggests that there can be overriding factors, perhaps something to do with weather, that influences the overall success of tick populations and, hence, the amount of grooming and hair damage and loss that will occur in those moose populations. Working in Isle Royale National Park, DelGiudice and co-workers (1997) agreed in part, stating that "nutritional restriction [stress] is related directly to preoccupation of infested moose with grooming...and effects of winter ticks on moose across geographic regions are primarily weather-dependent and density-independent".

Timmermann and Whitlaw (1992), citing a 1959 paper by Morris, stated that "often the major, common mortality factors may not be as important in influencing population fluctuations as those variable factors that operate inconsistently". Weather fits that category though this might change with the reality of global climate change and the now common back-to-back-to-back mild winters. Warmer, shorter winters may bode well for ticks in the north, but consequently, may not bode well for moose.

Very likely, both moose density and weather play major roles in influencing numbers of winter ticks in the environment. More research in this area is needed.

■ So what is a manager of the moose resource to do?

Moose are the largest members of the deer family in the world and one of the high-profile wild animals in Canada. Because of wise management and conservation, populations of moose in North America are doing well, very well indeed (FIGURE 9.5). Canadians relate to their moose, and moose are known by all, from grade school children to Prime Ministers.

FIGURE 9.5. Moose are free of ticks in summer. [LYLE FULLERTON].

Further, Canadians want to see healthy moose populations. So do moose biologists, which is why their management plans are usually aimed at maintaining or increasing viable, healthy moose populations.

Timmermann and Buss (1997) provided the following reasons for managing moose:

- They are magnificent animals, deserving of human attention and responsible treatment.
- They add beauty, diversity and interest to the environment.
- They are part of North America's wildlife heritage, and an integral part of a complex ecosystem.
- They have substantial recreational and economic values.
- They are an important source of food, particularly for subsistence users and native people.

Timmermann and Buss make it seem like moose are a wonderful renewable natural resource. They are.

Wildlife managers of the moose resource want abundant and healthy populations, and they want to be good stewards of the resource. Do they just live with winter ticks or is there something that can be done to lessen tick problems for moose? The following is true:

- tick problems are not going to go away, and tick-associated die-offs are going to occur periodically;
- thankfully, **winter ticks do not attack humans and do not affect the quality of the meat that is slated for consumption;**
- most moose populations seem to rebound following die-offs, some more quickly than others;
- even though a "ghost" is, by definition, dead, at least some, perhaps many, ghost moose survive. Not all ghost moose are on their last legs at winter's end;

- we can't do a lot about the weather.

Hence, the ongoing process of the adaptive "arms race". That said, as moose and tick numbers build, moose harvest by hunters is far more appropriate and humane than invasive harvest by winter ticks. We should be able to moderate some of the damage caused by winter ticks for moose by managing moose at below die-off levels.

To do that, numbers of moose in a particular area need to be known, with some precision, and changes in numbers over several years need to be documented. But moose are hard to count. They can be hard to see from the air in forested habitat, and are impossible to census from the ground (FIGURE 9.6). The population size and density of moose in specific areas are best determined by aerial survey in winter. This is, by far, the most practical and accurate method of estimating moose numbers. Weather conditions must be ideal and the specific counting technique used must be very accurate in its results.

The late Alaskan Bill Gasaway and colleagues devised the current "gold standard" aerial survey technique for moose in 1986. This technique, which is used in Alberta and many other jurisdictions,

FIGURE 9.6. Moose tend to be secretive and are difficult to census.

FIGURE 9.7. Aerial surveys in winter are the best and most practical way to determine numbers of moose. Here, a cow with her 9-month-old twins.

involves flying fairly large areas of generally continuous moose habitat. Variations in moose densities are determined by flying the same areas yearly, if possible (FIGURE 9.7).

Data acquired from aerial surveys, along with collection of information on habitat quality and quantity, and tick numbers, could be used to predict upcoming losses of moose. Appropriate harvest plans could be put in place that would reduce "boom-bust" changes in moose numbers to small changes over time, by harvesting more moose one-to-two years before predicted die-offs might occur.

Remember, winter ticks have no reason to conserve moose (see Chapter 8); that leaves it up to us. Conserve by better management practice.

There is a problem: aerial surveys are expensive. Using fixed-wing aircraft or helicopters for any wildlife activity has always been an expensive proposition, but with today's fuel costs, $1000 per hour of helicopter-use is probably the norm. Thus,

getting the most accurate data on yearly changes in numbers of any ungulate population in Alberta is, by default, expensive. Combine that with the fact that, in recent years, there has been insufficient investment in the management of our fabulous array of renewable wildlife resources, or their habitats. In relative terms, wildlife is not a high priority in much of Canada, at least if dollars dedicated to supporting wildlife programs—aerial surveys, doing research, acquiring more Fish and Wildlife officers, etc.—are the barometer of wildlife's priority.

The point is that, if we decided to manage moose so that they hosted fewer ticks, we could predictively set hunter harvest levels to avoid the "boom-bust" variations in moose numbers shown in Figure 9.2, and we would not feed our moose to the ticks. In other words, provide better data on moose densities for smaller areas over time, and harvest moose before the ticks do.

Epilogue

The farmer near Wabamun Lake had learned a lot about ghost moose during the few years he had been on the land. Disease and parasite information was part of the province's bow hunter education course, which he had taken when he decided that he needed some time away from the long hours of farming. He had taken up bow hunting, not that he had a lot of time to hunt, but he was thinking ahead, and planning for the time when his young son would come of hunting age. His father had done that for him, and it had given him a great sense of oneness with the land, his land. He was going to pass that on.

He had never quite gotten over finding the tick-infested ghost moose calf that had died on the property some 10 years before. He knew the area had plenty of moose and surmised that high densities of moose might influence parasites, such as those ticks. Some self-evident truths of farming cattle applied to moose as well. More animals in a small area means more chance of contact, and transmission of disease. Not exactly rocket science.

Yet, he had put up "no hunting" signs some years ago, as had many of his neighbours, in response to some hunter-related incidents, like leaving gates open and driving over his frozen fields without permission.

Then, a young fellow from Edmonton had stopped by one late-summer evening, seeking permission to put up some tree stands from which to bowhunt deer and moose. He explained that he was part of the "Hunting for Tomorrow Foundation's Youth Mentorship Program" that was getting first-time young hunters, mostly teenagers, into the woods and closer to nature. He also explained that the province had begun a program of trying to manage moose numbers better in some of the more highly populated areas, such as near Wabamun Lake. He would bring a new, young hunter to the farm and use hunting as a means to teach conservation, nature, the outdoors, etc. If he got permission, of course.

They hit it off, discussing their respective heritage that was tied to the land. The farmer gave permission for the young man to hunt his land. That fall there would be three bowhunters on the land where, in previous years, there had been only one.

This scene has been repeated more often in recent years in Alberta and elsewhere. Can we infer from it that the scourge of winter ticks is being influenced, and that moose populations in local areas will be healthier? Probably not, but perhaps this is a start. For certain, if nothing is done, winter ticks will remain the main hunters of moose.

How blood loss was estimated

■ Number of ticks on moose at winter's end:

Bull Moose:

Fifteen bull moose from central Alberta, examined between 1981 and 1989, had a median 19,714 ticks in March and April. Of that number, 27.6%, or 5441, were females.

Cow Moose:

Seventeen cow moose from central Alberta, examined between 1982 and 1989, had a median 17,560 ticks in March and April. Of that number, 18.0%, or 3161, were females.

Calf Moose:

Twelve calf moose from central Alberta, examined between 1982 and 1989, had a median 31,731 ticks in March and April. Of that number, 25.6%, or 8123, were females.

■ Compute blood loss due to tick bite:

1. Tick literature commonly suggests that adult ticks consume or process 2 to 3 times their blood-fed weight. To be conservative, assume that female winter ticks consume or process a volume of blood that is twice, rather than three times, their blood-fed weight.

2. Weights of blood-fed or engorged female winter ticks come from two sources of information. Vicky Glines (1983) studied winter ticks from central Alberta, the average weights of which were 0.61 grams. Ed Addison and colleagues (1998a) found weights of winter ticks from Ontario ranged from 0.81 to 0.88 grams. To be conservative, the lesser value, 0.61 grams, could be used.

   However, Drew and Samuel (1989) noted that the weight of engorged female ticks dropping from grooming moose, dropped gradually and significantly from early March to the end of April. In contrast, tick weights rose significantly in a moose that was sickly and did not groom. Since most or all moose groom in the wild, we assumed that grooming prevented all ticks from taking a complete blood meal before dropping from moose. Therefore, a more conservative weight, 0.50 grams, was chosen to use in the analysis.

   Remembering that 1 gram is equivalent to approximately 0.001 litre, blood loss in litres is as follows:

2 times engorged wt. females times number adult females on moose in March-April = blood loss in litres				
	Engorged wt. females	Number of adult females		Blood loss in litres
BULL MOOSE:				
2 X 0.50 grams X		5441	=	5.4 litres
COW MOOSE:				
2 X 0.50 grams X		3161	=	3.2 litres
CALF MOOSE:				
2 X 0.50 grams X		8123	=	8.1 litres

■ Body Weight of moose at winter's end:

In 1995, Gerry Lynch, moose biologist with the Alberta Fish and Wildlife Division, published December weights for bulls and cows from Elk Island National Park. Mean weights were 442 and 401 kilograms, respectively, for animals older than yearlings. March-April weights were assumed to be, conservatively, 10% less. Rounded figures used were 400 and 360 kilograms, respectively.

December average weights of bull calves (197 kilograms) and cow calves (171 kilograms) were averaged at 184 kilograms. March-April weights were assumed to be, conservatively, 5% less.

1. Bulls	▪ 400 kilograms at winter's end.
2. Cows	▪ 360 kilograms at winter's end.
3. Calves	▪ 175 kilograms at winter's end.

■ Estimated blood volumes of moose:

Blood volume for horses is estimated to be 8% to 10% of their body weight. Cameron and Luick (1972) estimated that monthly blood volumes for reindeer ranged from approximately 6% to 9% of body weight. Again, although one could go with 6%, 7%, etc., 8% will be used.

Even though the specific gravity of blood in, say, horses or cattle, is slightly higher (about 1.05) than water (1.0), it was assumed that 1 kilogram is roughly equivalent to 1 litre:

1. Bulls	▪ 400 kilograms X 0.08 = 32 litres
2. Cows	▪ 360 kilograms X 0.08 = 29 litres
3. Calves	▪ 175 kilograms X 0.08 = 14 litres

■ Summary:

Bulls must replace an estimated 5.4 litres of blood, or a minimum of 16.9% (5.4 litres/32 litres) of their blood volume, during late winter-early spring.

Cows must replace an estimated 3.2 litres blood, or a minimum of 11.0% (3.2 litres/29 litres) of their blood volume, during late winter-early spring.

Calves must replace an estimated 8.1 litres blood, or a minimum of 57.9% (8.1 liters/14 litres) of their blood volume, during late winter-early spring.

Bibliography

Aalangdong, O.I. 1994. Winter tick (*Dermacentor albipictus*) ecology and transmission in Elk Island National Park, Alberta. Master of Science thesis, Department of Zoology, University of Alberta, Edmonton, Alberta. 174 pp.

Addison, E. 1979. Report on mortality of Alfred Bog moose during March 1979. Unpublished Report, Maple, Ontario, 8 pp.

Addison, E.M., and R.F. McLaughlin. 1988. Growth and development of winter tick, *Dermacentor albipictus*, on moose, *Alces alces*. Journal of Parasitology, vol. 74: 670-678.

Addison, E.M., and R.F. McLaughlin. 1993. Seasonal variation and effects of winter ticks (*Dermacentor albipictus*) on consumption of food by captive moose (*Alces alces*) calves. Alces, vol. 29: 219-224.

Addison, E.M., R.D. Strickland, and D.J.H. Fraser. 1989. Gray jays, *Perisoreus canadensis*, and common ravens, *Corvus corax*, as predators of winter ticks, *Dermacentor albipictus*. The Canadian Field Naturalist, vol. 103: 406-408.

Addison, E.M., R.F. McLaughlin, and J.D. Broadfoot. 1994. Growth of moose calves (*Alces alces americana*) infested and uninfested with winter ticks (*Dermacentor albipictus*). Canadian Journal of Zoology, vol. 72: 1469-1476.

Addison, E.M., D.G. Joachim, R.F. McLaughlin, and D.J.H. Fraser. 1998a. Ovipositional development and fecundity of *Dermacentor albipictus* (Acari: Ixodidae) from moose. Alces, vol. 34: 165-172.

Addison, E.M., R.F. McLaughlin, and J.D. Broadfoot. 1998b. Effects of winter tick (*Dermacentor albipictus*) on blood characteristics of captive moose (*Alces alces*). Alces, vol. 34: 189-199.

Alexander, J.O'D. 1986. The physiology of itch. Parasitology Today, vol. 2: 345-351.

Anderson, R.C., and M.W. Lankester. 1974. Infectious and parasitic diseases and arthropod pests of moose in North America. Naturaliste canadien, vol. 101: 23-50.

Bassi, R. 1875. (Jaundiced verminous cachexy or pus of the stage caused by *Distoma magnum*). Medico Veterinario, vol. 4: 497-515. (Translated from Italian by G. Bonvini and published in 1963 in the Southeastern Veterinarian, vol. 14: 103-112)

Berg, W.E. 1975. Management implications of natural mortality of moose in northwestern Minnesota. Proceedings of the North American Moose Conference and Workshop, vol. 11: 332-342.

Bishop, F., and H.P. Wood. 1913. The biology of some North American ticks of the genus *Dermacentor*. Parasitology, vol. 6: 153-187.

Blyth, C.B. 1995. Dynamics of ungulate populations in Elk Island National Park. Master of Science thesis, Department of Agricultural, Food and Nutritional Science, University of Alberta, Edmonton, Alberta. 140 pp.

Blyth, C.B., and R.J. Hudson. 1987. A plan for the management of vegetation and ungulates, Elk Island National Park. Elk Island National Park and University of Alberta, Edmonton, Alberta. 398 pp.

Brown, J.H. 1944. The spotted fever and other Albertan ticks. Canadian Journal of Research, vol. 22: 36-51.

Brown, J.H., and G.M. Kohls. 1950. The ticks of Alberta with special reference to distribution. Canadian Journal of Research, vol. 28, 197-205.

Bruce, E.A. 1927. Entomological notes of veterinary interest. Proceedings of the Entomological Society of British Columbia, no. 24: 27.

Bubenik, A.B. 1997. Evolution, taxonomy and morphophysiology. Pp. 77-123, *in* Ecology and Management of the North American Moose, A Wildlife Management Institute Book, A.W. Franzmann and C.C. Schwartz (Editors). Smithsonian Institution Press, Washington, D.C., and London. 733 pp.

Burns, J.A. 1986. A 9000-year old wapiti (*Cervus elaphus*) skeleton from northern Alberta, and its implications for the Early Holocene environment. Géographie physique et Quaternaire, vol. 40, no. 1: 105-108.

Cameron, A.E., and J.S. Fulton. 1926-1927. A local outbreak of the winter or moose tick, *Dermacentor albipictus* Pack. (Ixodoidea) in Saskatchewan. Bulletin of Entomological Research, vol. 17: 249-257.

Cameron, R.D., and J.R. Luick. 1972. Seasonal changes in total body water, extracellular fluid, and blood volume in grazing reindeer. Canadian Journal of Zoology, vol. 50: 107-116.

Cowan, I.M. 1951. The diseases and parasites of big game mammals in western Canada. Report on the Proceedings of the 5th Annual British Columbia Game Conference, Victoria, British Columbia. Pp. 37-64.

DelGiudice, G.D., R.O. Peterson, and W.M. Samuel. 1997. Trends of winter nutritional restriction, ticks, and numbers of moose on Isle Royale. Journal of Wildlife Management, vol. 61: 895-903.

Drew, M.L., and W.M. Samuel. 1985. Factors affecting transmission of larval winter ticks, *Dermacentor albipictus* (Packard), to moose, *Alces alces* L., in Alberta, Canada. Journal of Wildlife Diseases, vol. 21: 274-282.

Drew, M.L., and W.M. Samuel. 1986. Reproduction of the winter tick, *Dermacentor albipictus*, under field conditions in Alberta, Canada. Canadian Journal of Zoology, vol. 64: 714-721.

Drew, M.L., and W.M. Samuel. 1989. Instar development and disengagement rate of engorged female winter ticks, *Dermacentor albipictus* (Acari: Ixodidae), following single- and trickle-exposure of moose (*Alces alces*). Experimental and Applied Acarology, vol. 6: 189-196.

Drew, M.L., W.M. Samuel, G. Lukiwski, and J. Willman. 1985. An evaluation of burning for control of winter ticks, *Dermacentor albipictus*, in central Alberta. Journal of Wildlife Diseases, vol. 21: 313-315.

Dymond, J.R., L.L. Snyder, and E.B.S. Logier. 1928. Number. 1: A faunal survey of the Lake Nipigon region, Ontario. Transactions of the Royal Canadian Institute, vol. 16, Part 2: 233-291.

Fenstermacher, R., and W. L. Jellison. 1933. Diseases affecting moose. University of Minnesota Agricultural Experiment Station Bulletin, no. 294. 20 pp.

Galloway, T.D. 2002. Getting to know your ticks. Blue Jay, vol. 60, no. 2: 107-112.

Garner, D.L., and M.L. Wilton. 1993. The potential role of winter tick (*Dermacentor albipictus*) in the dynamics of a south central Ontario moose population. Alces, vol. 29: 169-173.

Gasaway, W.C., S.D. Dubois, D.J. Reed, and S.J. Harbo. 1986. Estimating moose population parameters from aerial surveys. Biology Paper no. 22, University of Alaska-Fairbanks. 108 pp.

Gladney, W.J., O.H. Graham, J.L. Trevino, and S.E. Ernst. 1973. *Boophilus annulatus*: effect of host nutrition on development of female ticks. Journal of Medical Entomology, vol. 10: 123-130.

Glines, M.V. 1983. The winter tick, *Dermacentor albipictus* (Packard, 1896): Its life history, development at constant temperatures and physiological effects on moose, *Alces alces* L. Master of Science thesis, Department of Zoology, University of Alberta, Edmonton, Alberta. 143 pp.

Glines, M.V., and W.M. Samuel. 1989. Effect of *Dermacentor albipictus* (Acari: Ixodidae) on blood composition, weight gain and hair coat of moose, *Alces alces*. Experimental and Applied Acarology, vol. 6: 197-213.

Harington, C.R. 2003. Annotated Bibliography of Quaternary Vertebrates of Northern North America: with Radiocarbon Dates. D.R. Harington (Editor). University of Toronto Press, in collaboration with the Canadian Museum of Nature, Toronto, Ontario. 539 pp.

Hardy, C. 1869. Forest life in Acadia. Sketches of sport and natural history in the lower provinces of the Canadian dominion. London. (This reference was not seen. It was cited by Anderson and Lankester, 1974)

Hart, B.L., L.A. Hart, M.S. Mooring, and R. Olubayo. 1992. Biological basis of grooming behaviour in antelope: the body-size, vigilance and habitat principles. Animal Behaviour, vol. 44: 615-631.

Hatter, J. 1950. The moose of central British Columbia. Doctor of Philosophy thesis, Department of Zoology, The State College of Washington [now, Washington State University], Pullman, Washington. 356 pp.

Hays, W.J., and A.S. Packard. 1869. The moose tick. American Naturalist, vol. 2: 559.

Holmes, J.C. 1982. Impact of infectious disease agents on the population growth and geographical distribution of animals. Pp. 37-51, *in* Population Biology of Infectious Diseases, R.M. Anderson and R.M. May (Editors). Springer-Verlag, New York.

Holmes, J.C. 1996. Parasites as threats to biodiversity in shrinking ecosystems. Biodiversity and Conservation, vol. 5: 975-983.

Howard, C.W. 1917. New tick record for Minnesota. Journal of Economic Entomology, vol. 10: 560.

Karns, P.D. 1972. Minnesota's 1971 moose hunt: a preliminary report on the biological collections. Proceedings of the North American Moose Conference and Workshop, vol. 8: 115-123.

Kaufman, W.R. 1971. Role of the salivary gland in ion and water regulation during feeding in the female tick, *Dermacentor andersoni*. Doctor of Philosophy thesis, Department of Zoology, University of British Columbia, Vancouver, British Columbia. 260 pp.

Kaufman, W., and J.E. Phillips. 1973. Ion and water balance in the ixodid tick *Dermacentor andersoni*. I. Routes of ion and water excretion. Journal of Experimental Biology, vol. 58: 523-536.

Killick, Adam. 1999. Unusually high number of ticks may kill about 1,000 Manitoba moose. Itching drives them crazy. *National Post* newspaper, April 27.

Koch, J.G., and J.R. Sauer. 1984. Quantity of blood ingested by four species of hard ticks (Acari: Ixodidae) fed on domestic dogs. Annals of the Entomological Society of America, vol. 77: 142-146.

Lankester, M.W. 1987. Pests, Parasites and Diseases of Moose (*Alces alces*) in North America. Swedish Wildlife Research Supplement 1: 461-489.

Lankester, M.W. 2001. Extrapulmonary lungworms of cervids. Pp. 228-278, *in* Parasitic diseases of wild mammals, W.M. Samuel, M.J. Pybus and A.A. Kocan (Editors). Iowa State University Press, Ames, Iowa. 559 pp.

Lenarz, M.S. 1992. 1991-92 Aerial moose survey results. Unpublished report, Minnesota Department of Natural Resources, Wildlife Research, Grand Rapids, Minnesota. 8 pp.

Lothian, W.F. 1981. A history of Canada's national parks, vol. 4. Parks Canada, Ottawa, Ontario. 155 pp.

Lynch, G. 1995. Moose weights and measurements from Elk Island National Park, Canada. Alces, vol. 31: 199-207.

Mahoney, S.P. 2001. The land mammals of insular Newfoundland. The Antigonish Review, vol. 31, Issue 124: 87. (published by Saint Francis Xavier University and online at www.antigonishreview.com/)

McLaughlin, R.F., and E.M. Addison. 1986. Tick (*Dermacentor albipictus*)-induced winter hair-loss in captive moose (*Alces alces*). Journal of Wildlife Diseases, vol. 22: 501-510.

McPherson, M., A.W. Shostak, and W.M. Samuel. 2000. Climbing simulated vegetation to heights of ungulate hosts by larvae of *Dermacentor albipictus* (Packard) (Acari: Ixodidae). Journal of Medical Entomology, vol. 37: 114-120.

Mooring, M.S., and B.L. Hart. 1995. Costs of allogrooming in impala: distraction from vigilance. Animal Behaviour, vol. 49: 1414-1416.

Mooring, M.S., and P. J. Mundy. 1996. Factors influencing host selection by yellow-billed oxpeckers at Matobo National Park, Zimbabwe. African Journal of Ecology, vol. 34: 177-188.

Mooring, M.S., and W.M. Samuel. 1998a. The biological basis of grooming in moose (*Alces alces*): programmed versus stimulus-driven grooming. Animal Behaviour, vol. 56: 1561-1570.

Mooring, M.S., and W.M. Samuel. 1998b. Tick defense strategies in bison: the role of grooming and hair coat. Behaviour, vol. 69: 1-26.

Mooring, M.S., and W.M. Samuel. 1998c. Tick-removal grooming by elk (*Cervus elaphus*): testing the principles of the programmed-grooming hypothesis. Canadian Journal of Zoology, vol. 76: 740-750.

Mooring, M.S., and W.M. Samuel. 1999. Premature winter hair loss in free-ranging moose (*Alces alces*) infested with winter ticks (*Dermacentor albipictus*) is correlated with grooming rate. Canadian Journal of Zoology, vol. 77: 148-156.

Morris, R.F. 1959. Single factor analysis in population dynamics. Ecology, vol. 40: 580-588.

Murie, O.J. 1951. The elk of North America. The Stackpole Company, Harrisburg, Pennsylvania and the Wildlife Management Institute, Washington, D.C. 376 pp.

O'Gara, B.W., and R.G. Dundas. 2002. Distribution: past and present. Pp. 67-119, *in* Ecology and Management of the North American Elk, 2nd Edition, J.W. Thomas and D.E. Toweill (Editors). Smithsonian Institution Press, Washington, D.C. 962 pp.

Peterson, R.L. 1955. North American Moose. University of Toronto Press, Toronto, Ontario. 278 pp.

Peterson, R.O. 1990. Ecological studies of wolves on Isle Royale. Annual Report 1989-1990. Michigan Technological University, Houghton, Michigan. 14 pp.

Peterson, R.O. 1991. Ecological studies of wolves on Isle Royale. Annual Report 1990-1991. Michigan Technological University, Houghton, Michigan. 14 pp.

Peterson, R.O., and J.A. Vucetich. 2003. Ecological studies of wolves on Isle Royale. Annual Report 2002-2003. Michigan Technological University, Houghton, Michigan. 16 pp.

Pybus, M.J. 1999. Moose and ticks in Alberta: a dieoff in 1998/99. Occasional Paper no. 20, Fisheries and Wildlife Management Division, Edmonton, Alberta. 18 pp.

Pybus, M.J. 2001. Liver flukes. Pp. 121-149, *in* Parasitic diseases of wild mammals, W.M. Samuel, M.J. Pybus and A.A. Kocan (Editors). Iowa State University Press, Ames, Iowa. 559 pp.

Ritcey, R.W., and R.Y. Edwards. 1958. Parasites and diseases of the Wells Gray moose herd. Journal of Mammalogy, vol. 39: 139-145.

Samuel, B., and V. Crichton. 2003. Winter ticks and winter-spring losses of moose in Western Canada, 2002. The Moose Call, vol. 16: 15-16. January issue.

Samuel, W.M. 1988. Use of age classes of winter ticks on moose to determine time of death. Canadian Society of Forensic Science Journal, vol. 21: 54-59.

Samuel, W.M. 1991. Grooming by moose (*Alces alces*) infested with the winter tick, *Dermacentor albipictus* (Acari): a mechanism for premature loss of winter hair. Canadian Journal of Zoology, vol. 69: 1255-1260.

Samuel, W.M., and M. Barker. 1979. The winter tick, *Dermacentor albipictus* (Packard, 1869) on moose, *Alces alces* (L.), of central Alberta. Proceedings of the North American Moose Conference and Workshop, vol. 15: 303-348.

Samuel, W.M., M.J. Pybus, D.A. Welch, and C.J. Wilke. 1992. Elk as a potential host for meningeal worm: Implications for translocation. The Journal of Wildlife Management, vol. 56: 629-639.

Samuel, W.M., and D.A. Welch. 1991. Winter ticks on moose and other ungulates: factors influencing their population size. Alces, vol. 27: 169-182.

Samuel, W.M., D.A. Welch, and M.L. Drew. 1986. Shedding of the juvenile and winter hair coats of moose (*Alces alces*) with emphasis on the influence of the winter tick, *Dermacentor albipictus.* Alces, vol. 22: 345-360.

Seton, E.T. 1909. Lives of game animals. Volume III: Hoofed Animals. Doubleday, Doran and Company, Inc., Garden City, New York. 780 pp.

Skorupka, P.M. 1999. Some behavioural and physiological responses of free-ranging moose (*Alces alces*) to infestations of winter ticks (*Dermacentor albipictus*). Master of Science thesis, Department of Biological Sciences, University of Alberta, Edmonton, Alberta. 120 pp.

Stelfox, J.G. 1962. Liver, lungs, & larvae: Parasites and diseases in moose, deer and elk in Alberta. Land Forest Wildlife, vol. 5, no. 4: 5-12.

Sutherst, R.W., R.B. Floyd, A.S. Bourne, and J. J. Dallwitz. 1986. Cattle grazing behavior regulates tick populations. Experimentia, vol. 42: 194-196.

Telfer, E.S. 1984. Circumpolar distribution and habitat requirements of moose (*Alces alces*). Pp. 145-182, *in* Northern Ecology and Resource Management, R. Olson, R. Hastings, and F. Geddes (Editors). University of Alberta Press, Edmonton. 438 pp.

The Echo [newspaper for Athabasca, Alberta]. 1982. Ticks enter testimony, November 10, p. 7.

Timmermann, H.R., and M.E. (Mike) Buss. 1997. Population and harvest management. Pp. 559-615, *in* Ecology and Management of the North American Moose, A Wildlife Management Institute Book, A.W. Franzmann and C.C. Schwartz (Editors). Smithsonian Institution Press, Washington, D.C., and London. 733 pp.

Timmermann, H.R., and H.A. Whitlaw. 1992. Selective moose harvest in North Central Ontario-a progress report. Alces, vol. 28: 1-7.

Toronto Globe and Mail. 1983. Tick infestation killing B.C. moose, April 13, p. 10.

Trost, C.J. 1999. Black-billed Magpie (*Pica pica*). 28 pages, *in* The Birds of North America, no. 389, A. Poole and F. Gill (Editors). The Birds of North America, Inc., 1900 Benjamin Franklin Parkway, Philadelphia, Pennsylvania.

Wasel, S.M., W.M. Samuel, and V. Crichton. 2003. Distribution and ecology of meningeal worm, *Parelaphostrongylus tenuis* (Nematoda), in northcentral North America. Journal of Wildlife Diseases, vol. 39: 336-346.

Welch, D.A., and W.M. Samuel. 1989. Evaluation of random sampling for estimating density of winter ticks (*Dermacentor albipictus*) on moose (*Alces alces*) hides. International Journal of Parasitology, vol. 19: 691-693.

Welch, D.A., W.M. Samuel, and R.J. Hudson. 1990. Bioenergetic consequences of tick-induced alopecia on moose. Journal of Medical Entomology, vol. 27: 656-660.

Welch, D.A., W.M. Samuel, and C.J. Wilke. 1991. Suitability of moose, elk, mule deer and white-tailed deer as hosts for winter ticks (*Dermacentor albipictus*). Canadian Journal of Zoology, vol. 69: 2300-2305.

Wilkinson, P.R. 1967. The distribution of *Dermacentor* ticks in Canada in relation to bioclimatic zones. Canadian Journal of Zoology, vol. 43: 517-537.

Wilton, M.L., and D. L. Garner. 1993. Preliminary observations regarding mean April temperature as a possible predictor of tick-induced hair-loss on moose in south central Ontario, Canada. Alces, vol. 29: 197-200.

Zarnke, R.L., W.M. Samuel, A.W. Franzmann, and R. Barrett. 1990. Factors influencing the potential establishment of the winter tick (*Dermacentor albipictus*) in Alaska. Journal of Wildlife Diseases, vol. 26: 412-415.

Suggested Readings

Allan, S.A. 2001. Ticks (Class Arachnida: Order Acarina). Pp. 72 - 106, *in* Parasitic diseases of wild mammals, W.M. Samuel, M.J. Pybus and A.A. Kocan (Editors). Iowa State University Press, Ames, Iowa. 559 pp.

Alces. A scientific journal that publishes research articles on the biology and management of moose. See www.lakeheadu.ca/~alceswww/ alces.html Subscribe to: Lakehead University Bookstore, Lakehead University, 955 Oliver Road, Thunder Bay, Ontario P7B 5E1.

Franzmann, A.W., and C.C. Schwartz (Editors). 1997. Ecology and Management of the North American Moose, A Wildlife Management Institute Book, Smithsonian Institution Press, Washington, D.C., and London. 733 pp.

Kaufman, W.R. 1989. Tick-host interaction: A synthesis of current concepts. Parasitology Today, vol. 5, no. 2: 47-56. February issue.

Lankester, M.W., and W.M. Samuel. 1997. Pests, Parasites and Diseases. Pp. 479-517, *in* Ecology and Management of the North American Moose, A Wildlife Management Institute Book, A.W. Franzmann and C.C. Schwartz (Editors). Smithsonian Institution Press, Washington, D.C., and London. 733 pp.

Peterson, R.O. 1995. The Wolves of Isle Royale - A Broken Balance. Willow Creek Press, Minocqua, Wisconsin. 190 pp.

Rodgers, Art. 2001. Moose. World Life Library, Voyageur Press, Stillwater, Minnesota. 72 pp.

Samuel, W.M., M.S. Mooring, and O.I. Aalangdong. 2000. Adaptations of winter ticks (*Dermacentor albipictus*) to invade moose and moose to evade ticks. Alces, vol. 35: 183-195.

Schwartz, C.C., W.L. Regelin, A.W. Franzmann, and M. Hubbert. 1987. Nutritional energetics of moose. Swedish Wildlife Research Supplement no. 1: 265-280.

Sonenshine, Daniel E. 1991 and 1993. Biology of Ticks. Vols. 1 and 2, Oxford University Press, New York. 449 and 465 pp., respectively.

Stelfox, J.B. (Editor). 1993. Hoofed mammals of Alberta. Lone Pine Publishing, Edmonton, Alberta. 241 pp.

Strong, Paul. 1998. Wild Moose Country, NorthWord Press, Minnetonka, Minnesota. 160 pp.

The Moose Call Newsletter. A publication of the journal *Alces* (see page 93) that provides latest news in the moose world, and encourages members of the public to share their interest in moose.

Thomas, J.W., and D.E. Toweill (Editors). 2002. Ecology and Management of the North American Elk, 2nd Edition, A Wildlife Management Institute Book, Smithsonian Institution Press, Washington, D.C. 962 pp.

Thorne, E.T., E.S. Williams, W.M. Samuel, and T. P. Kistner. 2002. Diseases and Parasites. Pp. 351-387, *in* Ecology and Management of the North American Elk, 2nd Edition, J.W. Thomas and D.E. Toweill (Editors). Smithsonian Institution Press, Washington, D.C. 962 pp.

Acknowledgements

I am grateful to my colleague and friend, John Holmes, who paved the way for me to come to Alberta, then provided more than 25 years of encouragement, hunting partnership and ideas about how parasite ecology works. The insights, hard work and research results of graduate students Vicky Glines, Mark Drew, Dwight Welch, Oscar Aalangdong and Trish Skorupka, and postdoctoral fellow Mike Mooring are the "meat" of this book. I am proud of them, and their past and current accomplishments in life. Well done folks!

Many students, technicians (dare I say *tick*-nicians), and others, spent countless hours raising orphaned moose calves (a labour of love), and collecting data in the lab and field. I am glad that many went on to graduate school or veterinary school. Margaret Barker, Clarence Gerla, Brent Gray, Petr Komers, Michelle McPherson, Nadine Uhl and Chris Wilke deserve special thanks.

Staff and friends with Parks Canada, Elk Island National Park, have been supportive of, and participated in, our work on winter ticks since the late 1970s. I will not remember everyone involved, but the following made significant contributions to our studies: Fred Bamber, Chuck Blyth, Norm Cool, Fred Dixon, Ed Henderson, Rob Kaye, Bob Jones, George Lukiwski, Dennis Madsen, Brent McDougal, Wes Olsen and Jack Willman. Norm Cool, in particular, deserves special recognition; for 25 years he worked closely with me and my students and technicians. Thanks Norm!

Special thanks go to the many Fish and Wildlife officers and other Fish and Wildlife personnel who contributed to our research program over the years.

Many individuals contributed services, information, or both, for the book. Mike Mooring provided one idea after another the last 10 years. He is a remarkable person and scientist. Margo Pybus provided information about moose mortality, ticks for our research, photographs, editorial comments and much encouragement. Over the years, friends—Margo, Ed Addison, Vince Crichton and Murray Lankester—shared encouragement and their knowledge of moose and parasites of moose. Gerry Lynch did that and more, and also flew for countless hours, looking for ticky

With gratitude
BILL SAMUEL